The Best Spiritual Writing 2013

Edited by

PHILIP ZALESKI

Introduction by

STEPHEN PROTHERO

PENGUIN BOOKS

PENGUIN BOOKS

Published by the Penguin Group
Penguin Group (USA) Inc.,
375 Hudson Street, New York, New York 10014, U.S.A.
Penguin Group (Canada), 90 Eglinton Avenue East, Suite 700, Toronto,
Ontario, Canada M4P 2Y3 (a division of Pearson Penguin Canada Inc.)
Penguin Books Ltd, 80 Strand, London WC2R 0RL, England
Penguin Ireland, 25 St Stephen's Green, Dublin 2,
Ireland (a division of Penguin Books Ltd)
Penguin Group (Australia), 250 Camberwell Road, Camberwell,
Victoria 3124, Australia (a division of Pearson Australia Group Pty Ltd)
Penguin Books India Pvt Ltd, 11 Community Centre,
Panchsheel Park, New Delhi - 110 017, India
Penguin Group (NZ), 67 Apollo Drive, Rosedale, Auckland 0632,
New Zealand (a division of Pearson New Zealand Ltd)
Penguin Books (South Africa) (Pty) Ltd, 24 Sturdee Avenue,
Rosebank, Johannesburg 2196, South Africa

Penguin Books Ltd, Registered Offices:
80 Strand, London WC2R 0RL, England

First published in Penguin Books 2012

1 3 5 7 9 10 8 6 4 2

Selection and foreword copyright © Philip Zaleski, 2012
Introduction copyright © Stephen Prothero, 2012
All rights reserved

Pages 245–47 constitute an extension to this copyright page.

ISBN 978-0-14-312153-4
CIP data available

Printed in the United States of America
Set in Adobe Garamond Pro   •   Designed by Elke Sigal

Praise for
The Best Spiritual Writing Series

"Zaleski's compilation of spiritual writings restores 'best' to its rightful exceptional place. . . . It is a curious literary party at first glance, but the diverse forms, voices, topics, gradually coalesce into something bigger and more elegant, something spiritual and extraordinary." —*Publishers Weekly* (starred review)

"There is enough here to feed the hungry heart for years to come."
—Phyllis Tickle, author of *The Great Emergence*

"Illuminating . . . This anthology, as always, is a rich feast."
—*National Catholic Reporter*

"Outstanding . . . A beautiful collection for literary-minded readers of all religious persuasions."
—*Library Journal* (starred review)

"[A] luminous collection." —*Chicago Tribune*

"Like a very fine friend returned from a year's voyaging, laden with delights and treasures to share, Philip Zaleski brings us, here again, another trove of well-wrought, luminous, soul-bracing gifts." —Thomas Lynch, author of *The Undertaking*

"Those who embrace variety will find plenty to sink their teeth into." —*The Christian Science Monitor*

"[A] reliably bracing volume." —*Booklist* (starred review)

Contents

Foreword

AMONG THE LESSER MYSTERIES ASSOCIATED WITH GREAT SPIRI-
tual figures, there is this: that neither Jesus nor Buddha nor
Muhammad nor Confucius nor Pythagoras nor Socrates wrote a
book. Jesus once inscribed with his finger an undisclosed message
in the Jerusalem dust (John 8:6–8), and Muhammad, according
to a widely held Islamic tradition, received the entire Qur'an in
an instant from the angel Gabriel on the Night of Power, *lailat
al-qadar*, and spent the next twenty-three years giving voice to
this eternal, uncreated heavenly work. But none of the people
mentioned above, to my knowledge, wrote a book, a play, or even
a poem. And this is the least of it: for none of them, if the his-
torical record is to be trusted, practiced any art whatsoever. None
painted a picture, carved a sculpture, designed a building, or
played an instrument (with the single exception of Confucius,
who studied the *guqin*).

Why this reticence regarding art, among the truly great?
What does their reluctance tell us, as readers and writers, about
the nature and value of spiritual writing—or any art?

Each of these men had his own mission, method, and legacy.
To generalize about their common beliefs and practices is risky
business, inviting platitude, misrepresentation, and threadbare

syncretism. Instead, I will focus upon the figure most familiar to me, Jesus of Nazareth. The adopted son of a carpenter and perhaps one himself (Mark 6:3, Matthew 13:55), Jesus almost certainly was raised to appreciate proportion, grace, and elegance of design while learning his family craft. He had, we know, an eye for natural beauty, declaring of wild lilies that "even Solomon in all his glory was not arrayed like one of these" (Matthew 6:29). His literary skills were considerable, as we see in his brilliant parables and sayings. He spoke Aramaic, Hebrew, probably some Greek, perhaps some Latin, and was skilled at reading scripture. He lived in a community that esteemed the written word and rubbed shoulders with other cultures (notably Egyptian and Greco-Latin) that excelled in visual and literary arts.

Why then did Jesus never write a book? Numerous reasons come to mind—he had no inclination, he had no time, he had nothing to say—but they fit neither the man nor his mission. We must look for a deeper explanation. Luckily for us, a reliable guide is at hand, a man who illuminates whatever he surveys: Saint Thomas Aquinas, the greatest of Christian philosopher-theologians. In his *Summa Theologiae* (III.42.4), Thomas probes the question of Jesus's literary silence from a different angle, that of moral and spiritual obligation, asking not why Jesus (whom he always calls Christ) didn't write, but "whether Christ should have committed his doctrine to writing?"

To this question, Thomas responds in typically thorough manner, first advancing reasons why Christ should have written a book, then responding to these reasons, and in the course of this dialectic, explaining why Christ acted properly by never putting pen to paper. Christ should have written, Thomas conjectures, because "the purpose of writing is to hand down doctrine to posterity"; because the written Old Law of the Ten Commandments deserves a correspondingly written New Law of Christ; and because writing would "remove occasions of error . . . and open out the road to faith." These reasons, with the possible exception of the second, will strike most modern readers as sensible. So, too, will Thomas's commonsense counterarguments, for example, that Jesus didn't write because the apostles did his writing for him, and that anyone who rejects the testimony of the apostles will reject Christ's writings as well. But somehow this back-and-forth fails to satisfy; at times it seems trivial; one suspects that Jesus—a man whose every act had symbolic significance—refused to use his pen for more than practical reasons.

Happily, Thomas doesn't settle for these easy answers, but advances more profound reasons for Jesus's literary silence. One of the most important rests upon Jesus's dignity: "The more excellent the teacher," writes Thomas, "the more excellent should be his manner of teaching." Jesus, the highest and best of teachers, adopted the highest and best of pedagogies, that in which "His doctrine is imprinted on the hearts of His hearers; wherefore it is written (Matthew 7:29), 'He was teaching them as one having power.'" Thomas adds that this principle is not limited to Jesus, and he points out that "among the Gentiles Pythagoras and Socrates, who were teachers of great excellence, were unwilling to write anything." Great teachers, it seems, prefer oral instruction, with its intimate interaction between speaker and listener and its affinity for rhythm, rhyme, and parable.

A second reason for Jesus's refusal to write rests upon "the excellence of Christ's doctrine." Thomas cites here the Gospel of John, which states that if all that Jesus said and did had been written down, "the world itself, I think, would not be able to contain the books that should be written," an observation that Saint Augustine explains in this way: "We are not to believe that in respect of space the world could not contain them . . . but that by the capacity of the readers they could not be comprehended." In other words, what Jesus taught was too profound to be encapsulated in the written word. If he had inscribed his teachings, Thomas argues, "men would have had no deeper thought of His doctrine than that which appears on the surface of the writing." In Jesus's lessons however—as anyone knows who has tried to plumb his parables—the surface veils as well as displays. Thomas sums up this argument by quoting Saint Paul: "Christ's doctrine, which is 'the law of the spirit' . . . had to be 'written, not with ink, but with the Spirit of the living God; not in tables of stone, but in the fleshy tables of the heart.'"

What may we conclude from this? There seems no doubt that Jesus (and Muhammad, Buddha, Confucius, and the others) expressed, by what he did and by what he declined to do, a scale of values, in which the highest human activity is the enunciation and embodiment of truth. We are asked by all these teachers to move and to help others move from darkness to light, damnation to salvation, ignorance to illumination, self-centeredness to love. Art, it seems, is not the most important tool for accomplishing this task. What's worse, it can be a serious impediment. Socrates recounts in his *Apology* how, dismayed by the Delphic Oracle's declaration that he was "the wisest man in the world"—his chagrin occasioned, of course, by knowledge of his own ignorance—he sets out to find a wiser person among his fellow Greeks. When he comes to the poets, he discovers that "it is not wisdom that enabled them to write their poetry, but a kind of instinct or inspiration, such as you find in seers and prophets who deliver all their sublime messages without knowing in the least what they mean." What's more, this instinct fills them with unwarranted pride, for "the very fact that they were poets made them think that they had a perfect understanding of all other subjects, of which they were totally ignorant." Muhammad (or more properly, the Qur'an) also condemns poets, declaring that "as for poets, the erring follow them. Hast thou not seen how they stray in every valley, and how they say that which they do not?" (XXVI, 224–26). Such devaluation of art and artists is hardly limited to ancient thought, as Kierkegaard's celebrated ascent from the aesthetic to the ethical to the religious makes clear.

At first glance, all this may suggest that we do best to throw away our pens and paintbrushes, our violins and chisels. But the message isn't as dire as that. Socrates and Muhammad issue broadsides against poets, not poetry. The dialogues of Plato, Socrates's chief disciple, are masterpieces of world literature; and although the Qur'an emphasizes that Muhammad is a prophet, not a poet, that ancient scripture's rhymed verses forever set the course for Arabic literature and offer even today, in the words of its best English translator, Marmaduke Pickthall, an "inimitable symphony, the very sounds of which move men to tears and ecstasy." Beauty— wedded to, rather than indifferent to or divorced from, truth and goodness—remains a royal road to wisdom. Art has transported many an artist (and those who love and value the creations of artists) closer to God, as the lives and influence of Dante, Hildegard of Bingen, Fra Angelico, Palestrina, Bach, al-Ghazali, Rabi'a, Rumi, Kabir, Milarepa, Bashō, and countless others bear witness. The work of these people has one thing in common: it is *art in the service of eternity*, an art completely worthy of the name, an art that glorifies God while humbling the artist, a contemplative and moral enterprise whose aim—no matter how abstract its manner, harsh its voice, bitter its vision—is, as Dante enunciated in his letter to Can Grande, "to remove those living in this life from the state of misery and to lead them to the state of bliss."

To engage with this art, as creator or connoisseur, calls up the best in us. The rules of this engagement—how to make or receive "art in the service of eternity"—must be the subject of another essay. Here I'll only draw attention to one word in the above description: *service*. The artist is a servant, not a master; his stumbling block (as Socrates uncovered) is pride; his path is humility. With every stroke of pen or brush, he must remind himself to do his best to bring to light something better than himself. Writers or readers, painters or viewers, composers or listeners, we will never reach the bright precincts of eternity (whether or not we succeed in the dark halls of earthly "fame" and "reputation") if we do not see all art, including the splendid essays and poems that make up this volume, in proper perspective: as a mundane, valuable means toward a transcendent, invaluable goal.

I would like to thank Stephen Prothero, my agents Kim Witherspoon and David Forrer of Inkwell Management, and Carolyn Carlson, Amanda Brower, and the entire team at Penguin Books for their help and encouragement in assembling this volume. As always, I send a special thank you to Carol, John, and Andy, who remind me daily of why I pick up my pen.

PHILIP ZALESKI

Introduction

ONE OF THE UNWRITTEN RULES IN RELIGIOUS STUDIES IS THAT professors like me are supposed to separate our work lives from our faith (and doubt) lives. So when I am invited to give a sermon, I usually just say no right away. But for some reason when a small church in Massachusetts came calling a couple of years ago, I gave myself a while to think things over.

Perhaps it was the invitation, which came by e-mail from a minister who was out hiking with his family in Colorado. Perhaps it was the church, which this minister described as 30 percent "cheerful humanists," 50 percent "liberal Christians," and the remainder Buddhists, Jews, and assorted "others." But I suspect the real reason I finally said yes was that I was preparing some lectures on wandering, and this request seemed to be inviting me to wander into something new.

I began my first and only sermon by observing that wandering is a key theme in the world's religious and literary traditions: Abraham and Moses were wanderers, as were Jesus and Paul; Ulysses wanders for years across the pages of the Greek classic *The Odyssey;* the Pandavas wander almost as long across the pages of the massive Hindu epic the Mahabharata; and the Mesopotamian tale of Gilgamesh concerns a seemingly invulnerable god-man who makes a friend, a friend he loves, a friend who dies, whose death brings him grief, which grief sets him wandering. The gods may sit, I said, but to be human is to live between road and home, movement and rest, exile and return.

As I stood awkwardly in the pulpit, I tried to distinguish between wandering in the West and wandering in the East. Tucked inside western understandings of wandering is a sense of mischievousness slithering toward malfeasance, I observed. To wander, says the *New Oxford English Dictionary*, "is to turn aside from a purpose, from a determined course of conduct or train of thought; to digress; to pass out of the control of reason or conscience; to fall into error." It is, at Shakespeare's hand (in *Henry VIII*) to "wander from the good we aim at." It is in Lady Montague's confession that she has "so far wandered from the discipline of the Church of England as to have been last Sunday at the opera." Wandering, in short, is a bad thing. To wander is to wend your way into the wilderness (or the opera) far removed from the guidance of religious congregation and sacred scripture. It is to trade in productivity for play, to make common cause with fools and dreamers, to dance with the devil into the unknown. Or so goes the received wisdom.

Among Hindus and Buddhists, however, wandering is often seen not as punishment but as opportunity. How does Siddhārtha Gautama reach enlightenment? By deviating from the path of hard work and family values and wandering across the face of India. And what does the Buddha do after his Great Awakening? He wanders some more.

When I asked friends and family members for advice about my upcoming preaching debut, my daughters told me it didn't matter what I said. Sermons are boring, they said, so all that mattered was keeping it short. A colleague who preaches regularly told me to try to tell the truth. He also told me to focus on saying one (and only one) thing, which for me in that moment was this: If by fate or by Providence you happen to find yourself in a wandering way, try not to listen to the voices in your head telling you that wandering is wrong or wasteful. Nothing is going to die, and something might actually be born, if you turn off your computer, leave your "real work" behind, and go out on a wander without any particular purpose or destination in mind.

After the worship service I spent an hour or so talking with dozens of parishioners about their various desires for liberation from the purpose-driven life. A few months later I received a copy of a chapbook produced by the congregation—a series of meditations on wandering, one for each day in Lent.

I must confess to not knowing what spirituality really means, but it seems to me that there are a few things at play. At least as the term is popularly used, "spirituality" is often quite critical of "organized religion." It gravitates toward first-order experience rather than second-hand revelation, toward practice rather than dogma. In fact, those who describe themselves as "spiritual but not religious" often disdain their deep and ancient connections to the institutions, stories, and doctrines that gave their spiritual practices birth. In this regard, spirituality looks from my perspective like a sort of wandering itself—a deviation from the straight path of "organized religion" into the scary and exciting world that lies over the hill or around the bend.

"People wish to be settled; only as far as they are unsettled is there any hope for them," Ralph Waldo Emerson once wrote. And he was an unapologetic wanderer, who lit out for the Transcendentalist territories from his first life as a Unitarian minister. In his famous Divinity School Address at Harvard in 1838, he protested against "the famine of the churches." "Historical Christianity . . . has dwelt . . . with noxious exaggeration about the *person* of Jesus," he complained, and he urged the future ministers in his audience to dwell instead on something else. Nature, perhaps. Or the subtle self. Truth, Emerson said, "cannot be received at second hand." Each of us must experience it for ourselves.

Emerson largely restricted his wanders to the library and the lyceum circuit, but his friend Henry David Thoreau tramped out to Walden Pond, around Cape Cod, down the Merrimack River, and up Mount Katahdin in Maine. He also went much further than Emerson in cultivating a spiritual practice. Whereas Emerson read and reveled in Hindu and Buddhist literature, Thoreau worked to integrate into his life Asian spiritual disciplines. "To some extent, and at rare intervals," he wrote to a friend in 1849, "even I am a yogi."

In this way, Thoreau and Emerson invited today's "spiritual but not religious" folk to find their own paths. But the Transcendentalists were not the first Americans to try to cut through the icy rites and "corpse-cold" dogmas of their inherited religions to a deeper spiritual reality flowing underneath. The Puritans of the New England colonies, now widely disdained as prudes and hypocrites, were also spiritual practitioners par excellence. Ministers and parishioners alike sought to be shaken (and stirred) by the passion of Christ and the power of the Holy Spirit. In fact, in order to become a member of your local Congregationalist church in colonial New England, you needed to present an autobiographical "relation" of your spiritual journey that was moving enough to convince other church members you were likely of God's "elect."

All this is to say that "spirituality," at least in its commonplace meaning as a rebellion against "organized religion," is so suspiciously American that if it hadn't existed before 1776, Americans would have had to invent it. Perhaps, in a way, they did, taking earlier forms of spiritual experience and injecting into them the attitudes and assumptions of American culture. Individualism?

Check. Self-reliance? Check. Tolerance? Check. In this way, the Puritans begat the Transcendentalists who begat the Theosophists who begat the Beats who begat the counterculture who begat all of us (or at least those of us who read books like this).

Still, I have to say that the dichotomy between good "spirituality" and bad "religion" bequeathed to us by this venerable lineage of preachers and poets and ne'er-do-wells has never made much sense to me. Spirituality—whatever that word might mean—is not the opposite of religion but one of its many manifestations. After all, the great religions created and sustained most of the spiritual practices cultivated today by the "spiritual but not religious." Saint Teresa of Ávila, Saint John of the Cross, and other Catholics mystics were nurtured on the Catholic sacraments, and their works were read and remembered by priests and nuns. Without Islam, we would not have Rumi's poetry. Without Judaism, we would not have the Kabbalah. There would probably be mystics without the great religions, but we would not have heard of many of them.

This, by the way, is how Religious Studies professors write about the things we write about. We pride ourselves on dispassionate detachment—a historical observation here, some sociological analysis there. But we are humans too, and, like it or not, whatever spirit inhabits spirituality inhabits us as well.

My own writing on wandering came together when my life seemed to be falling apart. Previously, I had written a dissertation about American Buddhism and taught courses on American Hinduism. But I had kept my bodhisattvas and devas at a safe distance. As midlife overtook me, however, they started coming my way.

After a friend invited me to a gathering of a meditative dance community, I declined on the theory that I wasn't a good dancer. "Are you a good walker?" she asked. A few hours later I was hooked. Through that community, I made friends with the only real mystic I have ever known. And I eventually started attending (fitfully, alas) a Quaker meeting where, blessedly, no one ever talks. On a recent winter visit to my local meetinghouse, the only observable liturgy was the episodic work of an elderly man in denim overalls and sensible work gloves rising every fifteen minutes or so to stoke a wood fire. Here the gospel came and went in the rush of cold air over crackling oak. And at least to me it seemed to be saying, "First, do no harm."

The Best Spiritual Writing 2013 approaches spirituality the way many "spiritual but not religious" people approach the world's religions. No path is prescribed; inclusivity is the order of the day. There is poetry and there is prose. Authors are steeped in Catholicism or Protestantism, Judaism or Buddhism, and none of the above. There are autobiographical pieces that hit on that spirituality sweet spot of individual experience. But others read more like exercises in comparative religion or long-form journalism. And there are essays too, in Montaigne's sense of attempts, trial balloons, what-ifs—word wanders into the unknown.

Each spring at Boston University, I teach a "what-if" course called Death and Immortality. For more than a decade, I have had the pleasure of discussing with my students the greatest story ever told (the epic of Gilgamesh) and of reading with them from Plato's *Phaedo*, the Katha Upanishad, and the Book of Common Prayer. We try to figure out what Bill Murray's character in *Groundhog Day* has to teach us about reincarnation, and what we are supposed to take away from the last words of the Buddha ("All conditioned things are impermanent. Work out your own liberation with diligence").

The assumption of the course is that there is an intimate connection between how people understand the self (body only? soul only? some combination of the two?), dispose of the dead (cremation? burial? cryonics?), and imagine the afterlife (heaven? hell? moksha?). The course's conceit is that death is *the* question. As sociologist of religion Peter Berger has argued, the central challenge of every religion is to make sense of our mortality, so the religions that do that best do best in the long run. However, according to the feminist philosopher of religion Grace Jantzen, birth is an equally compelling question. Death is in many respects a man's game, she argues. For women, "generativity" (her word) is *the* question: How does something that did not exist a moment ago all of a sudden impress its existence upon us? Hindus have traditionally thrown a third question to the mix: What sustains things in the *bardo* between life and death we refer to as human existence? In this tradition, Shiva (the destroyer) explains death; Brahma (the creator) explains generativity; and Vishnu (the sustainer) explains how our lives (and the cosmos) keep spinning around and around.

Spirituality, it seems to me, responds to all three of these mysteries—how do things come into being, remain, and cease to be?—not so much in words as in experiences. We feel most alive, and most ourselves, when we are creating the things that matter to us. And when these things are dying we feel as if we are doing the same. But we also sense what the Sufis call the Really Real when we are in the midst of the things (or the beings) that sustain us.

I have already hinted that silence sustains me. But so do words: a new book; an essay that tries; a provocative sentence; a surprising turn of phrase; a word that emerges out of silence, hovers above it, and then floats away. Each of these mysterious things has a beginning, a middle, and an end. Each breathes of Brahma, Vishnu, Shiva. Each offers up a life (and death) of its own.

The essence of wandering is moving without destination into

the unknown, and opening yourself in the process to surprises. Though in rare cases wanderers do not return home, in most cases they do. So while there is no itinerary to wandering, there is a rhythm: escape, adventure, and return; out and around and back again. To wander is to find joy in small things, and to wrestle with big questions. It is to make choices rather than to follow rules. Should I take the shortcut or the long way around? Should I run or walk or sit or dance? You can wander alone, with a companion, or in a group. You can go by foot, train, car, or boat. And into deserts and woods, up mountains, over oceans. Wandering can happen on city streets. If you are limber enough, you can even wander up a tree. But you can also wander while reading, or writing, as long as you keep some eros in it, since close to the heart of wandering is letting go of means and ends, lingering in anticipation rather than racing toward the consummation of this or that.

In the pages that follow, authors flirt with angels and wander into sacred spaces. They look for love and speak of forgiveness. They interpret scripture, architecture, film. They remember to pray (and play). They confess their failures. They speak of evil and aging and zombies and art. Taking a cue from the Zen tradition— "chop wood, carry water"—these writers find the holy in the ugly, the extraordinary in the day-to-day, the rabbi in the custodian, the Great Goddess in the enteropathogenic bacteria of the Ganges. But none of this is particularly surprising. Neither is it surprising to encounter in these pages what may now be *the* dogma of spirituality: What is experienced cannot be said, and what is said cannot be experienced.

There are surprises in store, however. One blessed writer confesses a lack of interest in spirituality. Others invite us to wander out from our religious *and* spiritual routines, and then to bring our adventures back home.

It is commonplace to describe writing as a discipline, and

even a yoga of sorts. But these writers at their best turn our reading into a spiritual practice—an antidote to our purpose-driven culture, a circuitous route out of dichotomies such as effective and ineffective, productive and unproductive, good and bad, sacred and profane. To wander through this book is to wander with them into the cycles of life, death, and whatever (if anything) may lie beyond.

STEPHEN PROTHERO

COLEMAN BARKS

November Nights

FROM *The Georgia Review*

The last thirty years have brought a change to how
I work on writing. I used to like to go to a cabin
on Fightingtown Creek in Fannin County in
the north Georgia mountains. I used to work alone
for days, alternating between building a monumental
stone wall to keep the creek from eating out from under
the concrete block piers the house rests on, and letting
poems flow into shapes that often mention my adoration
of that creek's going by, and whatever it is flows around
and through us that that is metaphor for. Heraclitus
and I love to sit down up to the neck inside such music.
Company is more important now than ecstatic solitude.

At seventy-four, I have pretty much stopped stonework.
I keep thinking I am going back to it, but I don't act
on the thought. Almost every night now I walk
to this coffeehouse full of college students studying
and talking. Music playing. Johnny Cash tonight.
Lucinda. The students sing along with it so unself-
consciously. Uncivilized, almost primal. Oh, I used
to want a high-walled garden. Now I prefer a corner

in the open courtyard of a caravanserai well-used
by sugar merchants. Sometimes I sit up late-late
watching old movies and go to sleep in my chair.
I wake in sunlight at seven and go upstairs for proper
sleep in a bed, with my elaborate pillow arrangement.
I do so love these November nights that begin early
and last long, enormous, enveloping darks.
I have never considered suicide. Nothing is petty
or trivial, not really. It is a failure in my life that
I do not allot time to listen to classical music.
Mahler, Handel, Mozart, Beethoven. These would
maybe loosen new spontaneities in me, conversation
being the thing now, a kind of music to live inside.

Here you must hear now the opening of Mahler's
Ninth Symphony. The slight small sounds that seem
to be waiting and walking with us in an *andante
comodo*, the convenient ambling along that is
a slowing and starting up as something catches
interest for a moment in one or the other of us,
like music heard inside watersound, as I once did
by that creek in the cabin with such uncertain
foundations, a building chorale, Beethovenish, but
with even more majesty. It was so real that I walked
outside and started down the creekside path—it was
night—oddly imagining the Stuttgart Symphony
and Chorus might, most improbably, be camped
on the property next door. I soon turned back to sit
in the dark and fully hear the music that was rising
from within, as the practice of joy in my soul.

ANNIE BOUTELLE

The Calling of Saint Matthew

FROM *The Hudson Review*

by Caravaggio, 1599–1600, Contarelli Chapel,
S. Luigi dei Francesi, Rome

He thought it was going to be about
wealth, those five fat cats around the table,
glossy silk and velvet, their extravagant
plumed hats, as they count and shuffle
the coins—a world away from the two
strangers who stumble into the room
with their bare and dirty feet.

But perhaps it was about the body,
miracle of flesh?—the delicious boys
clustered around Matthew, whose
muscled columns of leg stretch out
under the table. Or all those hands,
soft and young, large and wrinkled,
busy pushing coins, or straightening
a lorgnette, or leaning on a shoulder
for protection. And Jesus's hand points
to Matthew, and Peter's follows—twin

puppets dancing above the table, each
pointed finger charged with the power
of a Sistine God reaching out to Adam.

Then it slammed into him—it was about
nothing else but that one tiny moment,
wrapped in light, the breathless time
when everything pauses, turns, slips.
And this is Matthew's only chance, no
need to ponder or weigh—as the dusty
golden light sweeps down on him, and
Jesus, still pointing, knows who will
follow, and turns his feet to the exit.

CARL DENNIS

New Year's Eve

FROM *The New Yorker*

However busy you are, you should still reserve
One evening a year for thinking about your double,
The man who took the curve on Conway Road
Too fast, given the icy patches that night,
But no faster than you did; the man whose car
When it slid through the shoulder
Happened to strike a girl walking alone
From a neighbor's party to her parents' farm,
While your car struck nothing more notable
Than a snowbank.

One evening for recalling how soon you transformed
Your accident into a comic tale
Told first at a body shop, for comparing
That hour of pleasure with his hour of pain
At the house of the stricken parents, and his many
Long afternoons at the Lutheran graveyard.

If nobody blames you for assuming your luck
Has something to do with your character,
Don't blame him for assuming that his misfortune

Is somehow deserved, that justice would be undone
If his extra grief was balanced later
By a portion of extra joy.

Lucky you, whose personal faith has widened
To include an angel assigned to protect you
From the usual outcome of heedless moments.
But this evening consider the angel he lives with,
The stern enforcer who drives the sinners
Out of the Garden with a flaming sword
And locks the gate.

BRIAN DOYLE

Let It Go

FROM *U.S. Catholic*

I'LL TELL YOU A STORY. FOUR YEARS AGO I SAT AT THE END OF MY bed at 3 in the morning, in tears, furious, frightened, exhausted, as drained and hopeless as I have ever been in this bruised and blessed world, at the very end of the end of my rope, and She spoke to me. I know it was Her. I have no words with which to tell you how sure I am that it was the Mother. Trust me.

Let it go, She said.

The words were clear, unambiguous, crisp, unadorned. They appeared whole and gentle and adamant in my mind, more clearly than if they had somehow been spoken in the dark salt of the room. I have never had words delivered to me so clearly and powerfully and yet so gently and patiently, never.

Let it go.

I did all the things you would do in that situation. I sat bolt upright. I looked around me. I listened for more words. I looked out the window to see if someone was standing in the garden talking to me through the window. I wondered for a second if my wife or children had spoken in their sleep. I waited for Her to say something more. She didn't speak again. The words hung sizzling in my mind for a long time and then faded. It's hard to explain. It's like they were lit and then the power slowly ebbed.

Let it go.

She knew how close I was to absolute utter despair, to a sort of madness, to a country in which many sweet and holy things would be broken, and She reached for me and cupped me in Her hand and spoke into the me of me and I will never forget Her voice until the day I die. I think about it every day. I hold those words close and turn them over and over and look at them in every light and from every angle.

For more than a year I told no one about this, not even my wife whom I love dearly and who has a heart bigger than a star, but then I told two friends, and I told them because they told me that they too had been Spoken to in moments of great darkness. A clan of the consoled, and there must be millions of us.

Billions.

We say a great deal about the Mother. We speak of her in Mass, in schools, in magazines and newspapers and newsletters and bulletins, in seminaries and schools, colleges and websites, and we know nothing of Whom we speak. All we know is a handful of stories from 2,000 years ago, shreds and shards, tattered threads from what must have been even then an unimaginable fabric. Miriam, she was named, and She lived, married, Bore Him, endured, wept over His icy corpse, died. When She died Her body rose into the heavens and vanished from earthly view.

But I tell you that She spoke to me one cold wet night in western Oregon, and Her words are burned on my heart as if She reached down with a finger like a sweet razor and traced them there at 3 in the morning, and I cannot explain how Her words changed everything and how there was the first part of my life and now there is the part after She spoke to me.

Let it go.

I still have a job and kids and my mysterious wife and a bad back and a nasal mutter and too many bills, nothing's changed outwardly, I didn't drop everything and hit the road hunched over in mooing prayer and song, and there are still all sorts of things quietly muddled and loudly screeching in my life, but something astonishing happened to me four years ago and it changed everything. Something broke and something healed, something so deep and joyous that I cannot find words for it, hard as I try.

We say a great deal about the Mother and we know nothing of Whom we speak. That is what I want to say to you. But She knows us. Trust me when I say that I know this to be true. Whatever else you hear today, whatever else you read, whatever else happens in your life, whatever way your heart is bruised and elevated today, remember that.

TERRY EAGLETON

The Nature of Evil

FROM *Tikkun*

THE DEVIL, SO THEY SAY, HAS ALL THE BEST TUNES, AND THIS seems to be the case when it comes to literature as well. Nobody would take a guided tour of Dante's *Paradiso* if they could have one of the *Inferno* instead. Milton's God sounds like a bureaucratic bore or constipated civil servant, while his Satan shimmers with mutinous life. Nobody would have an orange juice with Oliver Twist if they could have a beer with Fagin instead. So why is evil so sexy, and so profoundly glamorous? And why does virtue seem so boring? Why is it that when I told my thirteen-year-old son I was writing a book on evil, he replied "Wicked!"?

One answer, I think, is that it is not virtue that is boring but a particular, very familiar conception of it. Think of Aristotle's man of virtue, who lives more fully and richly than the vicious. For Aristotle, virtue is something you have to get good at, like playing the trombone or tolerating bores at sherry parties. Being a virtuous human being is a practice, like being a skilled diver or an accomplished tennis player; and those who are really brilliant at being human—what Christians call the saints—are the virtuosi of the moral sphere, the Pavarottis and Maradonas of virtue. Goodness in this Aristotelian view is a kind of prospering in the precarious affair of being human—a prospering which, if

Sigmund Freud is to be believed, none of us manages particularly well. The wicked are those who haven't developed the knack of fine living—those who botch the business, as you might make a mess of cooking an omelet or conducting a symphony orchestra. The wicked, then, are inept, crippled, deficient people who never really get the hang of human existence. They are like poor artists who can't knock themselves into shape. Whereas the good, the virtuous, are those who, like good artists, realize their powers, energies, and capacities to the full, in as diverse a way as possible. And because of this, they are brimming with life and high spirits. With this model, to ask "Why be good?" as people began to later, would be as ridiculous as asking "Why enjoy a dark, foaming, full-bodied pint of Guinness?" or "Why should a clock keep good time?" Virtue is a kind of energy or exuberance, which is why it is sometimes thought to have something to do with God. To say that God is good is not to say that he is remarkably well-behaved—most Christian theologians would not see God as a "moral" being at all—but rather that he is an infinite abyss of self-delighting energy, which no doubt means that he must have a boundless sense of humor as well (he needs one). For Christian theology, God is that abundant, overflowing, ecstatic *jouissance* at the heart of us, which is closer to us than we are to ourselves (as the unconscious is closer to us than the ego), and which allows us to be free and to flourish. To be entirely without such abundant, self-delighting life is to he evil; and this means that evil is not something positive but a kind of lack or defectiveness, a sort of nothingness or negativity, an inability to be truly alive. Evil may look lively, seductive, and flamboyant, but this is just the flashy show it puts on to cover up the hollowness at its heart. It is the paper-thinness of evil, its brittle unreality, which is most striking about it.

Whatever happened, then, to this ancient notion of goodness

as exciting, energetic, and exhilarating, and evil as empty, boring, and banal? Why do people now see things the other way around? One answer, at least in the West, is the gradual rise of the middle classes. As the middle classes came to exert their clammy grip on Western civilization, there was a gradual redefinition of virtue. Virtue now came to mean not energy and exuberance but prudence, thrift, meekness, chastity, temperance, long-headedness, industriousness, and so on. No wonder people prefer vampires. These may be admirable virtues, but they are not *exactly* exciting ones; and one effect of them is to make evil seem, by contrast, a lot more attractive, which is exactly what happened. Virtue had now become essentially negative. It was closely bound up with middle-class respectability. It had lost its sexiness and become restrictive rather than enabling. As Auden remarked of the Ten Commandments, there's no particular point in observing human nature and simply inserting a "not." We were now moving toward that perversion of moral thought (identified above all with the greatest of all modern philosophers, Immanuel Kant) for which virtue was all about duty, obligation, and responsibility, rather than in the first place a matter of finding out how to live fully, how to enjoy ourselves. Of course, duties, obligations, and responsibilities have their place in human life. What is disastrous is to place them at the center of one's moral vision. Duties and obligations make sense not in themselves, but in relation to the idea of living most fully and most richly. If they make that possible for the greatest number of people, well and good. But they are not to be seen as *definitive* of virtue. I say that virtue is really all about enjoying yourself, living fully; but of course it is far from obvious to us what living fully actually means. This is because, as we know from Freud and others, we are not transparent to ourselves as human beings. On the contrary, there is a sense in which we are desperately opaque to ourselves. So we can't just look inside ourselves and find the answers to these questions ready and waiting. Instead, we need special kinds of language, like moral philosophy and political theory, to help us in these matters. And the human conversation about what it is to live well—which is the answer to the question "what is morality?"—has never arrived at an agreed conclusion and probably never will. Astonishingly, we men and women of the modern age disagree on quite fundamental issues, which someone living in the Middle Ages might have found incomprehensible. We all agree that it is a bad idea to roast babies over fires, but we cannot agree on why we agree on this. And we probably never will. As long as we don't roast babies over fires, however, this may not matter too much.

Young people in the West these days have become very interested in zombies and vampires and other forms of the so-called Undead, and I think this has a bearing on what I am saying about good and evil. Zombies and vampires exist in some twilight, indeterminate zone between life and death, and the same is true of those who are evil. They can only manage a kind of sham, inauthentic life, a ghastly parody of genuine life; and they derive this life from their own sufferings and from the sufferings they inflict on others. This dreadful state of being is what it means to be in hell—though there cannot literally, actually be anyone in a place called hell, any more than you can be in a place called love or disgrace or despair. This is because for Christian theology there can be no life outside God, so nobody could reject God and still live. Hell means not perpetual punishment but absolute extinction. The fire of hell is God himself, with his relentless, terrifying, uncompromising love. God is a terrorist of love. And though this fire is the life and love of God, there are those who can't take this love (the wicked), who detest and despise it, and who are burnt to a cinder by it.

Only in being in atrocious pain can the evil persuade themselves that they are still alive. This is why they cling perversely to their sufferings, since without them they would be dead. They would rather cling to this obscene enjoyment of forcing others and themselves to suffer, which is a kind of nothingness, an inability to live truly, rather than risk the much more terrifying nothingness of abandoning themselves, in the faith that out of this kind of nothingness something positive, some new life, may finally emerge. The wicked are terrified of giving themselves away and cling to themselves for dear life as if to a lover.

This is why the damned or undead are said to be both despairing and exultant, miserable and mocking. They relish their agony because it is their only way of existing, and spit in God's eye because his ruthless, intolerable love risks removing their torment and along with it their identity. "I shit on your love!" William Golding's Pincher Martin snarls to his Creator. The damned are like an alcoholic who is so ravaged by drink that he can gain a spot of illusory relief only by stepping up his intake, thus shattering himself even more atrociously. Like the damned, the alcoholic is in the grip of what Freud called the death drive—and the true perversity of this drive is not that we are hell-bent on destroying ourselves, but that we do so because we are persuaded to take pleasure in the act of tearing ourselves apart. And that really is diabolical. The demonic is a kind of cosmic sulking, since comfort and forgiveness would be its undoing. The philosopher Kierkegaard sees the damned as those who refuse to relinquish their despair, since this would relieve them of their rebellious delight in rejecting Creation altogether. There is something adolescent about evil, and (as Saint Paul teaches) something grown-up about good. This is one reason why the image of children as good is so misleading (though the Victorians could never decide whether they were angels or demons, and needed them to be both). Children may be innocent, but that's not the same thing; and goodness is something they have to learn, to practice, to grow into. The Satanic, declares a character in Dostoevsky's novel *The Brothers Karamazov*, "demand that there be no God of life, that God destroy himself and all his Creation. And they shall burn everlastingly in the flames of their own hatred, and long for death and non-being. But death shall not be granted them."

The demonic are those who can't die because to do so would be to give up their terrifying drive to annihilate everything, including themselves. They are frightened of giving themselves away and cling to their anguish for dear life, as to a lover. They need to stay alive in a spectral kind of way in order to undo themselves and others. Only by spreading chaos and nothingnesss around themselves can they fill the frightful vacuum at the center of their being. Yet since this lack or absence at the center of our being is known as subjectivity, this is bound to be a doomed project. Only because there is something missing, repressed or lacking from us can we operate effectively. Only by negating non-being can the evil feel alive, yet non-being is both infinite and indestructible.

Those who cannot accept that there is a lack at the core of our being, or that this *manque d'être* is what makes us what we are, try to stuff this gaping wound with fetishes of all kinds—with doctrines, possessions, loved ones, sponge-rubber trousers, and so on. Fetishism for Freud is really a matter of trying to plug some fearful gap that is intolerable to you. The evil are those who cannot bear the fact that they are incomplete—which is to say, cannot bear the fact that they are human. They are pathological purists for whom matter itself is intolerably messy and indeterminate, and who are thus ascetic and virulently anti-materialist. The evil are precisely those who don't enjoy an orgy.

There is then, something deeply paradoxical about evil. The evil are those who can't stand nothingness, the nothingness that they are, and so try to cram this hole by creating even more nothingness around them, in the form of destruction. Only by trying to negate non-being can they feel alive, but non-being is infinite and indestructible. Nothing is more invulnerable than nothingness. And how do you know when you have destroyed it? The evil are those who quite often find this terrible nothingness (one that really lies at the heart of themselves) embodied in some alien, frightful figure outside themselves: the Jew, the Arab, the woman, the homosexual, the foreigner. But laying violent hands on those who embody negativity will not bring you any closer to murdering the non-being at the heart of yourself, since that lack is what makes us human in the first place.

The damned, then, are monstrous, Dracula-like travesties of the living. And the death drive that dominates them is equally a kind of travesty or parody of that terrifying force known as the will, with its indomitable, never-say-die passion to subjugate and possess, which even as I speak is wreaking havoc with millions of lives in the Middle East and Afghanistan in the name of Western ideals of progress and democracy. Freud himself had no doubt that within this drive or energy, which builds and destroys civilizations, lurked the death drive itself. This is profoundly ironic, since it means that concealed within our desire to create, to subdue to order, to reduce to harmony—in short, to overcome chaos (all very necessary, by the way)—lies a land of chaos itself. The will to order and dominate that yields us civilized existence is secretly in love with nothingness. There's something anarchic, out of hand, about our very lust for order and civility, vital though these things are.

This idea that death and dismemberment lie within the very impulse to exuberant life and the drive to build civilization was known to the ancient Greeks as the Dionysian, because Dionysus is life and death, Eros and Thanatos together, builder of cities and wrecker of them, both joy and destruction, affirmation and negativity. He is also for the ancient Greeks the patron of the greatest art form they bequeathed to the world: tragedy. Tragedy is the form that finds in our very capacity to confront chaos, to stare the Medusa's head of frailty and negativity squarely in the eyes, our capacity to go beyond it. Only by opening ourselves in this way to our own frailty and finitude might we have a chance for authentic life. Only by being hauled through hell might we have a chance of rising again. It is this that the evil cannot accept. They want to deny our frailty and negativity, not embrace it.

Tragedy is the form that recognizes that if a genuine human community is to be constituted, it can be only on the basis of our shared failure, frailty, and mortality. This is a community of repentance and forgiveness, and it represents everything that is the opposite of the American Dream. This means, in the terms of Jacques Lacan, that the symbolic can be founded only on the Real. Only by acknowledging the monstrous as lying at the very heart of ourselves, rather than projecting it outward onto others, can we establish anything more than a temporary, imaginary relationship with one another, one which is not likely to endure. This means relationships based on the recognition that at the very core of the self lies something profoundly strange to it, which is utterly impersonal and anonymous but closer to us than breathing, at once intimate and alien. This has had many names in Western civilization: God, Language, Desire, the Will, the Unconscious, the Real, and so on.

In the finest of all modern novels about life and death, Thomas Mann's *The Magic Mountain*, the hero Hans Castorp finally comes to see that the tenderness and comradeship he witnesses in his great Utopian vision in the Alpine snow is what it is only because there is a horror at its heart—the ritual sacrifice of a young child. All civilization is built on sacrifice, even if this is only the necessary repression of our more disruptive instincts. It is love, Hans comes to realize, not reason, which is stronger than death, and from that recognition alone can civilization flourish—but, the novel adds, "always in silent recognition of the blood sacrifice." Or as the poet Yeats puts it, "Nothing can be sole or whole that has not been rent." Sacrifice is the act by which the reviled, polluted thing, the pharmakos or scapegoat, undergoes the turbulent passage from weakness to power. It is only by identifying with this polluted, cast-out thing (which in early sacrifice usually involves eating it) that the city can be saved, that which is torn and bleeding can he made whole, justice can be accomplished, and life can be snatched from the jaws of death. This is why one of the modern names for ancient sacrifice is political revolution.

And so the death-dealing myths of Western modernity—the bad infinity of Faustian desire, which would annihilate the whole of Creation in its compulsive-obsessive hunt for the transcendental signifier, and which in doing so hubristically rejects all limits on the human enterprise and thus rejects death itself—must be countered by that other founding Western myth, the fable of Oedipus, who, blind and broken before Thebes, is finally forced to confront his own finitude and humanity, and who in doing so releases a great power for good. It is, if you like, a choice between two kinds of nothingness. On the one hand, the nothingness of the insatiable will, which overreaches itself and brings itself to nothing, and for which no actual object can be worth anything compared to the infinity that is itself. This (bad) infinity, one of whose modern names is desire, devalues everything sensuous and specific in its frantic search for all or nothing. Desire is absolutely nothing personal and will pass all the way through its (purely contingent) object in order finally to reunite with the only thing it really desires, namely itself. On the other hand there is that tragic acknowledgement of one's own inevitable failure and pollution, that peering into the pit of nothingness over the edge of which, so one hopes (but with absolutely no guarantees), something affirmative might finally crawl. Tragic humanism sees the need for this breaking and remaking, as liberal humanism does not. And this is in my view one of the most important ethical and political conflicts today.

Oedipus, the beggar king, stands before Athens. As he once returned an answer to the Sphinx, now his own presence poses a question to the city-state. Is it to gather this unclean thing, this stinking piece of nothingness, to its heart, or is it to cast it out as so much garbage? What is civilization to make of this ghastly parodic image of itself, at once stranger and brother, guilty and innocent, hunter and victim, man and monster, poison and cure, holy and defiled? "Am I now a man," Oedipus asks, "only when I am now no longer human?" It is a profound paradox he touches on here—that to be stripped of our culture and civilization, of all that makes for difference and specificity, is in one sense to cease to be human altogether, for it's this which constitutes our humanity; yet that in another sense nothing is more purely and simply human than this condition of utter dehumanization, that when we are stripped like Lear or the concentration camp victim of our cultural lendings to become less than human, we end up becoming more so. And then Theseus, ruler of Athens, takes an ethical leap into the unknown, inaugurating a radically original event. He welcomes the defiled beggar into the city, fearful of contamination but trusting that if he does so a great power for good will follow. That which is rejected is made the cornerstone; that which is cast out as so much excrement will prove to be fertilizing. As Oedipus is enshrined at the heart of the city, the violence that went into the making of civilization, but which then is always in danger of undermining it, is sublimated into a defense of the city itself. In a tragic action, only through self-emptying and dispossession can transcendence, risen life, be assured, and it is never really assured at all. It is not true, as the demented Lear snaps to his daughter, that nothing will come of nothing. On the contrary, the lesson of tragic humanism is that something will come only of nothing; and that those who fear that nothingness—those who refuse to acknowledge this thing of darkness as their own, who can see it only as a monstrous obscenity lurking on the threshold of their city-state—will themselves go to monstrous lengths to annihilate it.

ADAM GOPNIK

Life Studies

FROM *The New Yorker*

WHEN I WAS IN THE MIDDLE OF THE JOURNEY OF MY LIFE, I
decided to learn to draw. No, I wasn't lost in a dark, enclosing for-
est, but it *was* the Manhattan equivalent: a midweek dinner party
that had turned the corner to eleven-thirty and now seemed likely
never to end at all. The host was a terrific cook, but one of those
seven-course terrific cooks, disappearing into the kitchen for a
quarter of an hour at a time to execute the latest Ferran Adrià rec-
ipe, while we all secretly gripped the underside of the dinner ta-
ble, realizing that the babysitter meter was running and we would
have to be up again in six hours to dress the kids and get them to
school.

Having exhausted the exhausted neighbors to my left and
right during the previous course breaks, I turned at last to my
neighbor across the table. I knew that we had kids in the same
school, and that he was married to the woman beside me. He
was curly-haired and handsome in the pugilistic way that looks
as though it ought to include a broken tooth. I asked him what
he did.

"I'm an artist," he said. "A teacher. I teach people how to
draw." He spoke with what I would come to recognize as a diffi-
dence touched by, well, touchiness.

"Would you teach me how to draw?" I asked, for reasons that at the moment seemed as clear-flying as a lark in spring air, but that, over the next two years, receded and rose mysteriously, like fish swimming in a muddy aquarium.

"Sure," he said, only a little surprised. "Come by the studio." His name was Jacob Collins, and he explained that he supervised an "atelier" in midtown, called the Grand Central Academy of Art.

I said that I was going off to California to speak on Manet—did I intend that to be credentialing? I suppose I did—but that I would certainly come the week after.

He seemed to stiffen, even wince, at the mention of the French painter's name. I might have said the man who painted the poker-playing dogs.

"You don't like Manet?" I said, wondering. Didn't everybody like Manet?

"Actually, I—" he began brutally, and then I thought I saw his wife, across the table, shoot him a "Don't start!" look, and he shrugged.

This was interesting. The realists I knew in the art world defended their occupation the way the religious believers I know defend theirs, as one more spiritual option within the liberal system: *See, I'm just exploring the possibilities of pluralism.* This was clearly something else. This guy really didn't like Manet!

When I got back from California, I armed myself with a sketchbook and a set of pencils and went to visit the Grand Central Academy of Art. The academy was in the same midtown building as the Mechanics Institute Library, a favorite retreat of mine already. I climbed the creaky wooden stairs, took a step into the atelier, and blinked. I was in a series of rooms that could have been found in Paris at the Académie in 1855 or, for that matter, in Rome in 1780. Easels everywhere, and among them plaster casts of classical statues, improbably white and grave and well-muscled and oversized. The statues weren't displayed, as they are at the Met, at dignified intervals, but bunched together, higgledy-piggledy, so that the effect was that of a cocktail party of tall white plaster people who worked out a lot. The Discus Thrower frowned and threw his discus; a Venus wrapped herself up, modestly, an Apollo looked toward the Korean delis and salad bars just below; an incomplete David, with his slingshot, gazed into the distance. The scene was almost too much like one's mental image of it, as though a student interested in New York politics had opened the door to a downtown clubhouse and found corpulent, cigar-smoking politicians in porkpie hats and short-hemmed pants and vests with "Tammany" written in bleeding type across them.

A cluster of students in mildly worn jeans worked on their drawings. Each hand moved, back and forth, up and down from the wrist, and the world seemed to flow onto the sketcher's paper like silver water taking the form of things seen, subtle gradations of gray and black that didn't just notate the things in an expressive shorthand but actually mirrored them, in a different medium and on a different scale.

Jacob had someone set me up with an easel, and then gave me a small plaster cast of an eye—something taken from a statue perhaps three times life size. "Just try and copy that," he said.

I held my pencil tight and began. I had a graduate degree in art history, and I *liked* to draw, though I did it very badly. I could make crude line-drawing faces, which, depending on the direction of the "eyebrows," might register vanity, conceit, worry, or anger. A squiggled line, for instance, drawn as a girl's eyes, looks like self-delight. If the hieroglyphs of emotion were that simple, how much harder, my modern-art-trained mind demanded, could the work of representation, mere mirroring, really be?

I stabbed at the paper, trying to copy the contour of the plaster eye, and then looked at what I had done. I had just made a hard line that limped awkwardly along the top of the page, enclosing a kind of egg shape, meant to be the pupil. I looked at the easels around me, at the play of shadow and shade, the real look of the thing, which seemed so natural. I flipped a page in my notebook and, gripping my pencil tighter and staring back at the eye, tried again. It was even worse, like a football inside a pair of parentheses.

After two more flipped pages, Jacob came over. In a gentle tone very different from his dinner-party manner, he said. "Yes, well . . . I would argue that the space you're asserting here in this corner could be seen as something much spacier. I think you could allow these intervals to . . ." He struggled for words. "To breathe more, without betraying the thing you're drawing." It was the most elaborately polite way possible of saying that the circle on the page meant to indicate the pupil was way too big in relation to the ridiculous double line meant to represent the orbit.

I started over on a new page, and tried to stare the damn thing down. The plaster eye looked back at me opaquely, unforgivingly. I took a deep breath and tried to let my hand, follow the line in front of me. But how did you distinguish the raised bits of the eye from the hollow bits, the ups from the downs? The light fell across the thing, creating darks and lights, but how to register these with a pencil point? I tried crosshatched shapes in the darker corners, but this made the eye look like a badly wrought Mayan numeral over which someone had scribbled tic-tac-toe boards. My chest tightened, and my breath came short. It was impossible.

As I crossed Sixth Avenue two hours later, I was filled with feelings of helplessness and stupidity and impotence that I had not experienced since elementary school. Why was I so unable to do something so painfully simple? Whatever sense of professional competence we feel in adult life is less the sum of accomplishment than the absence of impossibility: it's really our relief at no longer having to do things we were never any good at doing in the first place—relief at never again having to dissect a frog or memorize the periodic table.

Or having to make a drawing that looks like the thing you're drawing. I hadn't learned to draw because I had never been any good at drawing. Now I knew that I never would be. I tried to forget about the morning, and when I saw Jacob in the halls of our kids' school I exchanged brief, hooded embarrassed looks with him, as one might with a failed blind date.

The little urge that had made me want to learn to draw was still intact, though, and, for the next six months, tugged on my insides like a bad conscience. Partly it was simple curiosity. *How do they do that trick?* Another reason was compensatory. For all the years I'd spent talking about pictures, the truth was that I had no real idea of how to draw or of what it felt like to do it. I would mistrust a poetry critic who couldn't produce a rhyming couplet. Could one write about art with no idea how to draw? It was true that the art I had written about was mostly of a kind that had stored life drawing away in the attic, as a youthful relic from summer camp. The older I got, though, the more I was pulled toward pure craft, unalloyed accuracy, the struggle to translate the surface of the world into a sentence or a sketch. And if I was going to study this thing I wanted to go there with a real hard-ass.

Still, I would have let the plan to learn drawing molder in the pile of my unfulfilled ambitions—the pile that sits on the desk of life right next to the pile of escaped obligations—had I not bumped into Jacob one day at our kids' school, trapped in a corridor as he waited for a conference.

"Hey," he said. "If you're still interested, why don't you come around to my studio sometime and watch while I draw? We can just talk." And so that Friday I went over to his studio to watch him draw.

It was an old renovated stable and, in décor, was like a smaller version of the atelier—classical busts on shelves and even a hanging skeleton—but more intimate, and with Jacob's own sober paintings (a genial-looking older man, beautiful half-torsos of grave young women, a Berkshire winter landscape or two) hanging above our heads. There was a black Lab, who nuzzled visitors, and slept, and barked loudly when someone came to the door. Instead of the fluorescents of the atelier, there were jerry-rigged spots, small lamps clamped as needed to wooden pillars to throw a narrow tunnel of warm light on the object to be drawn, or, set wide, to make the light come raking across the model.

I liked it there, a lot. So, for the next year or so, I went often to the studio on Friday afternoons, and kept Jacob company as he drew in semi-darkness. Sometimes there was a skull or bust to draw, sometimes a naked person stretched out on a platform up front. I had an easel, to be sure, and would make a mark or two as I watched him work.

Jacob drew and drew and drew. His paintings had a sombre, melancholic cast, in the manner of Thomas Eakins. But his drawings were prestidigitations, magical evocations of the thing seen, pencil drawings as accurate as photographs but with the ability that a photograph lacks to distinguish the essentials. He drew still-lifes, nudes, and portraits in the same timeless, distilled style.

And yet they were far from flowing or automatic. Week after week, the same sitter or skull was lit in place, and, though the act of drawing would go on, you would sometimes wonder when it would *happen*. He made minimal progress from hour to hour, but never left his station. Watching Jacob draw was a bit like watching a climber on a sheer rockface, slowly trying out one crampon and then another, looking for a foothold, advancing a couple of feet and then spending the night on the rockface in his bag, upright— albeit a climber engaged in a steady conversation with a friend on the lost art of true rock climbing.

"I always wanted to be doing this," he said, meaning drawing in the classical style. "And I couldn't understand why the world wouldn't see it as legitimate. I drew from when I was really, really small—anything, comic books, Spider-Man. And then, when I started in art school, the attitude was 'That's great, so good, and, you know, pretty soon you'll outgrow this!' " He laughed. Jacob was always trying to strike a decent mean between affirmation of his secret faith that art had been going wrong since the eighteen-sixties and his desire not to get caught up in the reactionary grievance-keeping that disfigured much of the revivalist world he lived in. "You'll outgrow wanting to draw the world as it is, search-ing for this beauty, this place where light and the body meet—that was the attitude of most of the art teachers I had," he went on. "So I had to re-create a world in which I could do the kind of drawing I wanted to do. I wasn't alone in this. There were quite a few of us trying, and, bit by bit, and book by book, and practice by practice, we tried to remake the world of atelier realism that had been dis-carded and abandoned." Over time, he assembled a group of teachers and students and enthusiasts, all given over to the practice of classical drawing from life and plaster casts, and from that nu-cleus came this studio and then the Grand Central Academy.

As in any marginal community, there were, I learned, fierce schisms and expulsions. I say marginal; it was marginal to me, but it wasn't marginal to the people in it. Micro-worlds don't look micro to the microbes. (And what we think are macro worlds don't look macro to the next biggest thing up; Apollo smiles down from Parnassus on career retrospectives at MOMA.) Like all subcultures, this was a complete society, with rules and rivalries. Jacob referred disdainfully to "Tomming realists," by which he meant realist artists who bowed and scraped before the masters of the avant-garde plantation, apologizing for their practice and just asking for the freedom to hoe a few acres of representational oats. Jacob was Nat Turner: he didn't want his own back forty; he wanted the keys to the big house.

Sometimes we would talk about our kids, and sometimes about music—he loved to play Bellini and Verdi in the studio, and was trying to master string trios with his son and daughter. It was only when we talked about art that we disagreed: he hated the triumph of modernism, and I did not, and there were moments when I felt a bit like a lapsed Roman Catholic who, out looking for a good Unitarian to show him a new spiritual path, has found instead a cheerful, welcoming Satanist, though one with a black Lab and kids at the same school. Jacob wanted to rid his language of any taint of the age of the avant-garde. "I don't even know what to call what I do," he said. " 'Realism' is the obvious name, but realism is a specific thing from modern art, all that Courbet-derived stuff, meaning the primacy of belonging to the world out there, and being accepted as an agitator. It's sort of the *opposite* of what I'm after. 'Traditionalism' is O.K., because it's based on lost traditions, but that makes it sound too much like just repeating something older. Neo-traditionalist? How can something traditional be neo?" The best half-serious label he could find was "traditional realist revivalism," and he had to admit that it still wasn't very good. He knew that you couldn't erase history; on the other hand, what if history was all wrong? "You can't go back," he said once, sighing. "I know that. But you can *look* back."

Over the weeks of listening and watching, I began at last to draw the thing in front of me, or to try to. Jacob had made one adjustment in what might generously be called my "technique." Instead of holding the pencil tight and stabbing away, I was to hold it underhand, and make large sweeping, fencing-like gestures that might block out the general shape of whatever it was we were looking at. And then he told me to place an imaginary clock face on top of those first broad, easy underhand gestures.

"Just make tilts in time," he said. "Imagine that there's a clock overlaying what you're drawing. Then make one tilt on the clock, then check to see if it matches up with what you see, look to see if it's at the proper angle on the clock face, and then correct it. Make it the right time. Now, there, you've got that line"— a descending scrawl meant to indicate the upper slope of a skull we were drawing—"and it's at, oh, what would you say, twelve-ten? I mean in relation to the vertical axis."

He stepped back and looked at my easel. "I would argue that, if you look at it again, the time on this clock is really much closer to twelve-eleven, or twelve-twelve. . . ." He trailed off and looked fiercely at the page.

"Twelve-thirteen?" I said, not wanting to seem completely blind.

"Yeah! Maybe you're right. Twelve-thirteen." Then he said, formally, "That's an inquiry I'd like to pursue," and erased my line and let me add another, two degrees lower.

Nothing had prepared me for how one could fix a line merely by rubbing it out and implanting another line a bare thirty-second of an inch above or below. The choice of the first line could be freely made, unbounded, improvisational. For you could always erase and remake; the eraser was the best friend a would-be artist had. And the erased line, still barely visible beneath, had an eloquence of its own, since it smudged the space in a way that suggested pentimenti, second thoughts, a hazy penumbra of light and shadow. Light leaks into the world, and an erased line with a line above suggests that leakage. Nothing in a graduate degree in art history prepares you for the eloquence of the eraser.

I looked again at the erased space and the new scrawl. To my shock, it did have the faintest impress of anatomy, of organic life, of the way a jaw actually joins a skull.

"Yeah," Jacob said, nodding, as he looked at the new lean of the line, and touching my shoulder as though my pencil had somehow just spat out a Raphael cartoon. He cheered up and went back to his own easel. "Now don't worry about, you know, drawing or art. Just draw that clock hand in your head, one contour meeting the next, and ask, What time is it between them?" And so for hours, weeks, that's what I tried to do. I wasn't really drawing. But at least I was making tilts in time.

You can't go back, but you can look back, Jacob had said, and certainly he looked, and saw, for himself. We went to a show of Bronzino drawings at the Met, and I expected him to be impressed. Who was a greater master of classical drawing than Bronzino?

But Jacob was struck by how quickly Bronzino had settled on his solutions. "Well, now, he has this kind of model in his head, a formula. He sees a child and he sees these orbs." He gestured. "Three of them. Three balls, intersecting like pawnbrokers' balls: chubby legs, chubby chest, chubby head, and *boom*—a cherub." He made three quick circles with his right hand, and the typical form of a Bronzino cherub was written briefly in the air. "Do you notice how he has so much mastery of certain areas, and then he has the solution to others ready in his head?" He looked harder at the face of a Madonna, and sighed. "There's a smoothness, a slightly comic-book-complacent solution, to his chins and ears."

We walked on and scrutinized a couple of well-muscled torsos. "You know, you can tell when someone's really *looking* at a body by the absence of parallel dents. When a person is standing or resting, the dent on one side of the body is usually met by a fullness on the other. When you get these two dents"—he pointed to what he meant—"it looks sort of stylish, but it's not really true, and you sense that. You rarely get a model whose rib cage is so clearly articulated and whole."

Looking at these beautiful drawings, I now realized that they were not found visions, or lines of poetry: they were made of tacit compromises between agreed-on fictions and hard-sought facts. Bronzino was called a mannerist not because that was where he happened to fall in the metaphysical chess game called "art history" but because he really had a manner. It was made of double dents and triple cherubic circles. Some fight between the ideal and the real, far from being a Neoplatonic abstraction, was actually going on in each drawing: when it tipped too far toward the ideal, it became a cartoon and lifeless; tip it too narrowly toward the actual, and it lost all the poetic sweep of the Grand Manner. The more you instructed yourself about the risks—the tussle of sight and muscle and bone—the more you appreciated the triumphs. The thing itself was argued out inch by inch on the page, not a foot or two above or just beside it, on the label.

We came at last to a small, unspectacular drawing of an old man. "I think this is the best drawing here," Jacob said. "Look how he's worried his way through that head, through the wrinkles— he's looking all the time in this one, and not letting his hand do the thinking for him."

At the end of the show, we stepped back out into the hall of the Met. "I can't say I'm too impressed by old Bronzino," Jacob said. "There aren't a lot of great drawings in there."

There was a mix-and-match show of Met drawings and prints on the way to the stairs, and we looked at an Alex Katz. Jacob made a face. It did look smooth, generalized, conceptualized, and simplified to the point of vacuity. Of course, I told myself, that was the point—to be smooth, stenographic, and direct—but for the moment I luxuriated in the originality of a shocked response.

"The *suckiness* of it," Jacob said. "I want my drawing not to suck." He was goading me, just a little, I knew, with a half smile somewhere six levels down.

"It's a style," I said. "Deliberately smooth and simple."

"Simple, because who needs good?" he teased. We inched toward an Andrea Mantegna, a bizarre engraving from the early fourteen-seventies of Silenus, the hideous and yet entrancing fat man. Jacob stopped.

"That is *great*!" he murmured. "I used to keep a Mantegna up in the studio just for hope. I mean, look at that." I knew the Mantegna was great, but, for the first time, I thought I saw *why* it was great: the discipline of drawing in play with an instinctive feeling for form, an unwillingness to compromise on what a fat drunken old oracle would look like—those rolls on his thighs, the three chins, not neat orbs of cherub-chubbiness but real human lard—intermeshed with the dignity of myth. My hand tingled at the thought of trying to draw that way. I had always loved Mantegna, liked Alex Katz, enjoyed Bronzino; but now I understood that the intuitions had arguments, that the feelings were matched by facts. A drawing was a surface of minute claims and compromises and clichés—some places where the received or even idealized wisdom was accepted and some places where it was argued out and a new truth arrived at.

We stopped for coffee afterward, and I asked Jacob why, given his skill at seeing and showing the world as it was, he never wanted to draw the particulars of *this* world as it is, the world that we found ourselves in, where people met at endless dinner parties. He drew his kids, beautifully, but without their iPods and Game

Boys and VitaminWaters. Why not draw as a novelist might write, with the appurtenances and accessories of this time?

He looked at me and seemed almost angry. "No, that's— you've so absorbed the premises of modern realism into your head that you can't see past it. Why didn't Michelangelo draw people buying fish, instead of nudes and gods? He was looking for some idea of beauty, rooted in this world"—he made a gesture around the coffee shop, taking in everything, light and time and the human forms seated there—"that didn't need an iPod to justify it. He really had an idea of timeless beauty. Why is beauty less interesting to you than journalism?"

Although I found the certainty of Jacob's exclusions odd, they had their resonance. I had come to feel not just inadequate as an art critic, in the absence of any skill, but also alienated from art in its current guise. Learning to draw was my way of confronting my disillusion with some of the louder sonorities and certitudes of the art with which I had grown up and for which I had once been a fierce advocate. For, surely, if there was absurdity in writing about art without being able to draw, there was even more comedy in valuing craft and praising mere cunning—in finding yourself trying to write skillfully about the purposefully skill-less. I could recite by heart the catechism: art had in the past century emancipated itself from mere description, and cultivated an expertise less artisanal but no less demanding—conceptual, historically conscious, made of mind and thought. Over the years, however, the absence of true skill—the skill to do something with your fingers at the command of your mind, which can be done only by a few, after long practice—unmanned my love, and that created a problem for me. I could parse, and praise, a Jeff Koons fabrication or a Bruce Nauman video, but was I really in love with things so remote from the ancient daily struggle to make something look like something else? Someone out of sorts with the practice of an art form can still be a critic; someone out of sorts with the premise of an art form is merely a scold. A jazz critic who does not like improvisation does not like jazz. Yet I was still happiest in museums, and thought I might remember why by learning to draw.

The funny thing was that Jacob knew the catechism, too. I had been shocked to discover that a portrait that hung near his easel was of Meyer Schapiro, one of a handful of art historians who had invented the humanist appreciation of abstract art, and, it turned out, Jacob's great-uncle. Jacob knew the score. But what if he was right, and the whole thing had been a mistake, and we all had to start over from scratch, or at least from a sketch? It was a possibility worth looking at.

Later that week in the studio, there was a nude model, a perfectly muscled young man named Nate. Jacob made another correction in my drawing. He had me hold the pencil underhand again, and start by making sweeping, open guesses at the form, and then looking at the imaginary clock, erasing the off lines, correcting, making tilts in time.

But, as I stared into the impossible landscape of ripples and nubs and shadows in Nate's torso, Jacob said, "Look into his torso and find a new form, another shape to draw. Something outside your symbol set."

I looked puzzled, and he explained, "I mean, don't draw a chest, or what you think a chest looks like. The ideas you've got in your head about the way things look—get rid of them. Find something else in there to draw. Find a dog. The outline of some small African nation. A face." He came around to hover over my shoulder. "See there, right in the space beneath his breastbone, I see this kind of snooty-looking butler, his chin pointing out and his nose in the air and his eyes half shut. Do you see him?" I squinted and looked, and then I did. Sort of: a face implicit in the accidents of light and shadow and flesh.

"O.K. Just draw the butler with the side of your pencil, shade by shade, and you'll be drawing him." He gestured toward Nate. "Draw the snooty butler, and you'll start a solid passage."

I learned to burrow in, underhand, eraser at the ready, searching for swelled-up bullfrogs and smiling bats and butlers with their noses in the air and all the other odd shapes that the play of light on flesh produced. The way out was, homeopathically, the way back in: lose your schematic conventions by finding some surprising symbol or shape in the welter of shades, and draw that. Here was the brain's natural language of representation, as Leonardo knew, when he counselled artists, in the first true break toward life drawing, to look at the patterns of moss on cave walls and visualize clouds.

The ultimate kitsch representation of art-making is the moment in the movie "The Agony and the Ecstasy" when Charlton Heston's Michelangelo, desperate to break his symbol set of divine likenesses, sees the nebulous form of God creating Adam in the clouds above his head. Now I saw that this scoffed-at scene is a purely pragmatic image of creativity: Michelangelo needed to break through his symbol set by finding new shapes to look at. Searching in the clouds for figures is the most rational course for an avid and alert artist to follow. We can't know if he saw his ceiling in the clouds, but he may have squinted and tried to see clouds, or butlers, in his ceiling.

Why do life drawings look like life? Why do these collections of shrewdly borrowed shapes and broken lines strike us as real? After all, what is presented to our retina when we look at the bleached skull or the five and a half feet of naked person—the particular riot of color and light reflections, pink and white and dark—looks nothing like the six inches of orderly silver-to-black line marks on ivory paper. Even line itself, the assertion of a contour, however nuanced and optical the shadings within, is as fictional as a quotation mark. The process, as the Bronzino drawings showed, must involve some play of the "conceptual" (the shapes we know) and the "perceptual" (the shades we see). But how?

One view, which lingers in the social sciences, though it was long ago discarded in psychology, is that the language of line drawing is all conceptual, as artificial and in need of being learned as the Egyptian hieroglyphs. Yet every honest observer senses that a life drawing, no matter how many pawnbrokers' balls and snooty butlers it includes, has an edge of persuasive illusion. My drawings of Nate didn't look like Nate because that's what drawings of Nate look like. They looked like Nate because, however ineptly, they showed something of the way Nate looked.

Drawing has conventions, though. What counts as convincing now isn't the same as what counted as convincing in medieval times. In the twentieth century, E. H. Gombrich argued that in drawings conventions always interact with perceptual information: "schemas," conventional symbolic images, come first, and then we correct them bit by bit as we observe and adjust them to life.

But it now seems possible that the tonal drawing is the mind's first draft. In the nineteen-seventies, the cognitive psychologist David Marr formalized the idea that, in effect, we see the real world first as a series of life drawings, as a shaded play of light falling on the world—what Marr called, half jokingly, a "two-and-a-half-dimensional sketch," a field of cells that represents information about a surface or an edge. Yet those mental sketches are of no use unless they're corralled by higher-level frames into discrete, fixed shapes—into exactly the "symbol set" that Jacob was trying to get me to discard. Some of those frames help to orient us in space, distinguish up from down and left from right, but some are more richly symbolic: they help us sort out recurring forms from mere incidents of light. We turn shades into shapes, and then shapes into symbols.

The new view is that our Western life-drawing tradition is a neat bit of cognitive jujitsu; the sophisticated "optical" rendering of generalized regions and nuanced shade actually represents the more "primitive" mental map. It took Leonardo and Raphael to show us what the mind's eye sees first—regions and shadings, instead of conceptual shapes and things—while every cartoonist shows us what it sees second. In fact, the new idea suggests that life drawing is less an acquired instrument of slow-crawling craft, and more just something back there that we delve deep to find again. This may in turn help explain the enduring mystery of why the oldest of all human representations, the cave paintings of Altamira, Lascaux, and Chauvet, are expertly rendered as shaded, three-dimensional life drawings, full of persuasive highlight and shadow. The caveman in us still draws what he sees, until the Egyptian in us interferes. (Certain language-disabled kids can make drawings that seem precociously optical, and, where people used to claim that the emergence of art is proof of symbolic, language-based culture, the psychologist Nicholas Humphrey has argued that the existence of the perfectly modulated cave paintings suggests that the people who made them didn't yet know how to talk.)

Yet the "symbolic frames" that organize our representation of vision don't seem to be hardwired; they change all the time. We can learn to draw from life, but we can also learn to understand those abstract funny faces, with their movable eyebrows. This is why, though what visual psychology can say about drawing is rich, what it can say about art is limited. Symbolic games aren't set. The seeing mind, or the drawing hand, is like a dealer in a poker game, who, as the players get bored with five-card draw or seven-card stud, calls out a new variant: now lowest hand triumphs; now deuces are wild; now the highest hand and the lowest hand both can take the pot. A cartoonish Philip Guston scrawl or a slick John Currin contour can both be winners.

Drawing is one of those things which sit on the uneasy and bending line between instinct and instruction, where seeming perversity eventually trumps pleasure as the card players and the kibbitzers interact and new thrills are sought. And this truth was the source of Jacob's discontent. His real dream, I saw, was to drive the kibbitzers from the temple of card playing, as mine was to become a card player, not a kibbitzer. But, in truth, kibbitzers and card players, observers and artists, shades and shapes and symbols are all parts of a single game, shuffled together in the big bluff we call culture. Without the card players, as Jacob knew, there was no skill in the game, but without the kibbitzers there was no skin in it, no point to watching. In fact, without the kibbitzers you couldn't even call the activity a game, more just an obsession—which, at times, is what it seemed to be for Jacob, and for me.

For a few months, I had been searching for strange shapes to break my symbol set. One day, when Nate was posing, I began to make quick stabs, and sketches. I saw a kind of hamster with soft rabbit ears where his shoulder joined his arm, its blunt snout pressing toward the eyes, and I tentatively drew that. I was following the image, doing sight-system checking, sketching the animal shapes, making tilts in time, rubbing out the weaker lines and letting the better ones bloom . . . and, miraculously, the outline of an arm appeared, and a shoulder, and it all looked more or less right.

It was a terrible drawing, I knew, but it was not a conceptual schema of an arm and shoulder. It was some recognizable rendering of the pattern of light in front of me. Jacob came over and said, "Yeah, that's got some of the shape. I would argue that you could erase here just slightly." It was, as I say, a terrible drawing—the core was way too wide, so that I had given Nate a Herculean expanse of torso, way out of proportion to the arms—but the relation between arm and shoulder was almost human, almost recognizably true. It was the best thing I had ever drawn, and I realized that I hadn't drawn it as I had imagined, God's hand finally resting on mine to steal a true contour from the world. No, I had made it up out of small, stale parts and constant reapplications of energy and observation, back and forth. I stood back. The good bit was about two and a half inches long, and no good at all by any standard. But it was a stab at a shape seen, at a pattern of incoming light and shade that made a shape. I was drawing.

In truth, the rhythm of fragment and frustration, of erasure and error and slow emergence of form, was familiar. I'd hoped the drawing would be an experience of resistance and sudden yielding, like the first time you make love, where first it's strange and then it's great, and afterward always the same. Instead, drawing turned out to be like every other skill you acquire: skating, sauce-making, guitar playing. Ugly bits slowly built up, discouragingly not at all like what you want, until it is. You learn, laboriously, the thumping octave bass with the chord two octaves above, and suddenly you are playing "Martha My Dear" and then you have it and you play along with the record and are half sad and half happy: that's all the magic of it? The bad news, I was finding out, was that drawing was just like everything else you learned to do. The good news was that drawing was like everything else, and even I could learn to do it.

. . .

There was one missing piece left to discover, though. One Friday I went to the studio to draw, and there was a naked woman there. We had been drawing Nate, and Nate was fine—but Anna was *gorgeous*, red-headed and voluptuous, and I swallowed hard as I set out to stare at her and find a frog or a snooty butler or a newly independent African nation in the burrows and hollows of her body.

"Hi," she said when I came in. She looked bored beyond words, though she chewed gum with a thoughtful, rhythmic grace. I had just come back from a parent-teacher conference, and Jacob and I talked briefly about fifth-grade curriculums.

"Our kids go to the same school," I called out to Anna, who was posing under the hot spotlight. She moved her red hair away from her face, and readjusted her torso.

"Yeah, so I gather," she said. She had an old-fashioned, Seventh Avenue accent.

I stared between her breasts innocently, virtuously—and found, at last, a spaniel on its back, its paws in the air. (My kids had just got a dog.) I began to touch and erase and touch again, and Anna's body took shape under my pencil. Jacob came over and corrected my drawing. I had mismeasured the proportions between breast and pubis. "Measurement is so essential," he said. He explained that we always make heads and hands oversized, and fill in the middle, as though the places of maximum sensory attention naturally demand the most attention. But I still couldn't get the proportions of Anna's torso right. So, as Jacob had taught me, I held my hands up in a small square to adjust the "sight-size"—making both the thing seen and the thing drawn fit into the same square—and then, in frustration, held a thumb out and squinted with one eye so that I could have an easier measure of the distance, as I saw it. Hands in small square, thumb out, and squinting—my God, I was acting like every artist in every silent movie I had ever seen!

Jacob came over and looked at my nude. "You've got this too far down." He pointed to the light-gray haze I meant for her pubic triangle. It should have been much higher up. I erased and began to adjust. "You've centered it, because in your symbol set that's where it belongs. Look again." I moved the little triangular schema up and over.

"Her nipples, you've got them centered, too," Jacob said. "They are at angles akimbo to each other. Look at the angle. Tell time." I pushed one nipple a smidge off center, and left the other one alone, and then made the pubic triangle more like the bicycle-seat shape it really was. Suddenly, she was alive—right there on the page! I had a flick of desire for a mark I had just made on a page with a pencil. Appetite drives drawing; that's what makes sure that there is no such thing as abstract art. I stepped back. It was not just closer to the truth but sexy, real, my own paltry Galatea.

Anna came over and looked. She was obviously disappointed. It was still a pretty crappy drawing. But then I saw her as she was, which was neither as she was on the couch nor as she was on my paper. She was tiny. I am a small man, but she came up to my shoulder. There she was on the page, though, as voluptuously large as a Matisse model. Jacob laughed. "There's a fiction part of what we do, too," he said. The truest drawing is the most feigning, and no help for it.

Jacob turned his drawing of Anna into a painting, and it is the centerpiece of his new exhibition at the Adelson Gallery. In the painting, she looks sultry, pained, a Rubens version of an Andrew Wyeth mistress. I can hear the art historians of the future speculating sapiently on her mood, her melancholy, even on her relation to the painter.

I stepped away from the studio after the year. I still like to draw, but the questions that I had come with were mostly answered, or at least quieted, which in life is pretty much the same thing. Drawing, I now think, need not be the bones of art, but skill must always be the skeleton of accomplishment. Without the one right tilt in true spatial time, there's nothing to see. And that's so even if the skill is cerebral, the time told abstract. Our (reluctant) admiration goes to people who can do things we can't. We know we can't do them when we try and fail.

Art without accomplishment becomes a form of faith, sustained more by the intensity of its common practice than by the pleasure it gives to its adherents in private. That it fills the habit of faith—makes communities, encourages values, creates hierarchies—is perhaps the best thing about it. The strongest argument for religion is not that it is in touch with God but that it puts us in touch with one another. The best argument for an art that no one can entirely like is that it makes us like one another more.

For the time being, the world remains its own drawing; we walk a tightrope above an abyss, and the grace of the walk does not deny the artificiality of the wire. I know now that there is no straight line that you can draw around a circumstance to take its shape away, there are only marks, made underhand, that you erase and adjust and erase again, over and over, until the black dog barks and the afternoon is over, and you close your pad and call it life.

JESSICA GREENBAUM

No Ideas but in Things

FROM *The New Yorker*

We checked the vents and hidden apertures of the house,
then ran out of ideas of where it might be open to the world.
So we couldn't figure out how the squirrel was getting in.
We each had methods that succeeded in shooing him,
or her, out the door—but none of them lasted. Whether
it was the same squirrel—terrified when in the house, and
persistently so—or various we couldn't tell because,
tipped off by a glance, he zigzagged from froze-to-vapor,
vanishing, Zorro-like, until signs would tell us he had
revisited the sideboard to dig in the begonia. (Escaping
Newcastle in a search for coal.) We plotted his counter-
escape, laying a path of pecans to a window opening
on the yard. A few days would pass, and, believing him
gone, we felt inexplicably better than when we began.
Then, from another room, the amplified skritch of nutmeg
being grated—and, crash. Bracelets off dresser tops, bud
vases, candy dishes, things houses have that the backyard
doesn't. You don't think of squirrels knocking things over,
but inside it was like living with the Ghost and Mrs. Muir.

When we couldn't trust the quiet or prove his absence,
we cast him as that hapless shade: worry. Our own gray
area, scat-trailing proof of feral anxiety. But after a few
cycles of release-and-catch I grew bored with the idea,
with its untamed projections. Since he dashes up walls,
(yanked, like a pulley), or seeks treasure in a five-inch pot,
daily, why not adopt him as optimism's travelling rep?
I tried. But the sun comes up, we step toward the stove,
and he shoots out like a cue ball, banks off the kitchen door
—what mayhem is caused by going to make coffee!—
and the day, again, begins with a shriek. We are now in
week three and I accept that, inside, the squirrel is going
to stand for something else. And so is the May rain
and so is the day you took off your coat and the tulips
joined in with the cherry blossoms and the people came out
and the pear-tree petals floated down in polka dots
around the tulips, and even around the cars. We name life
in relation to whatever we step out from when we
open the door, and whatever comes back in on its own.

MALCOLM GUITE

Antiphons

FROM *Christianity and Literature*

In Memory of Andrew Dickson

> Hope is an orientation of the spirit, an orientation of
> the heart; it transcends the world that is immediately
> experienced, and is anchored somewhere beyond its
> horizons . . . It is not the conviction that something
> will turn out well, but the certainty that something
> makes sense, regardless of how it turns out.
>
> —VACLAV HAVEL

O Sapientia, quae ex ore Altissimi prodiisti,
attingens a fine usque ad finem,
fortiter suaviterque disponens omnia:
veni ad docendum nos viam prudentiae.

> *O Wisdom, coming forth from the mouth of*
> *the Most High,*
> *reaching from one end to the other mightily,*
> *and sweetly, ordering all things:*
> *Come and teach us the way of prudence.*

O Sapientia

I cannot think unless I have been thought,
Nor can I speak unless I have been spoken.
I cannot teach except as I am taught,
Or break the bread except as I am broken.
O Mind behind the mind through which I seek,
O Light within the light by which I see,
O Word beneath the words with which I speak,
O founding, unfound Wisdom, finding me,
O sounding Song whose depth is sounding me,
O Memory of time, reminding me,
My Ground of Being, always grounding me,
My Maker's Bounding Line, defining me,
Come, hidden Wisdom, come with all you bring,
Come to me now, disguised as everything.

O Adonai, et Dux domus Israel,
qui Moysi in igne flammae rubi apparuisti,
et ei in Sina legem dedisti:
veni ad redimendum nos in brachio extento.

> *O Adonai, and leader of the House of Israel,*
> *who appeared to Moses in the fire of the burning*
> *bush*
> *and gave him the law on Sinai:*
> *Come and redeem us with an outstretched arm.*

O Adonai

Unsayable, you chose to speak one tongue,
Unseeable, you gave yourself away,
The Adonai, the Tetragramaton
Grew by a wayside in the light of day.
O you who dared to be a tribal God,
To own a language, people and a place,
Who chose to be exploited and betrayed,
If so you might be met with face to face,
Come to us here, who would not find you there,
Who chose to know the skin and not the pith,
Who heard no more than thunder in the air,
Who marked the mere events and not the myth.
Touch the bare branches of our unbelief
And blaze again like fire in every leaf.

O Radix Jesse, qui stas in signum populorum,
super quem continebunt reges os suum,
quem Gentes deprecabuntur:
veni ad liberandum nos, jam noli tardare.

> *O Root of Jesse, standing*
> *as a sign among the peoples,*
> *before you kings will shut their mouths,*
> *to you the nations will make their prayer:*
> *Come and deliver us, and delay no longer.*

O Radix

All of us sprung from one deep-hidden seed,
Rose from a root invisible to all.
We knew the virtues once of every weed,
But, severed from the roots of ritual,
We surf the surface of a wide-screen world
And find no virtue in the virtual.
We shrivel on the edges of a wood
Whose heart we once inhabited in love,
Now we have need of you, forgotten Root,
The stock and stem of every living thing
Whom once we worshiped in the sacred grove,
For now is winter, now is withering
Unless we let you root us deep within,
Under the ground of being, graft us in.

O Clavis David, et sceptrum domus Israel;
qui aperis, et nemo claudit;
claudis, et nemo aperit:
veni, et educ vinctum de domo carceris,
sedentem in tenebris, et umbra mortis.

O Key of David and sceptre of the House of
Israel;
you open and no one can shut;
you shut and no one can open:
Come and lead the prisoners from the prison
house,
those who dwell in darkness and the shadow
of death.

O Clavis

Even in the darkness where I sit
And huddle in the midst of misery
I can remember freedom, but forget
That every lock must answer to a key,
That each dark clasp, sharp and intricate,
Must find a counter-clasp to meet its guard,
Particular, exact and intimate,
The clutch and catch that meshes with its ward.

I cry out for the key I threw away
That turned and over turned with certain touch
And with the lovely lifting of a latch
Opened my darkness to the light of day.

O come again, come quickly, set me free
Cut to the quick to fit, the master key.

O Oriens, splendor lucis aeternae,
et sol justitiae:
veni, et illumina sedentes
in tenebris, et umbra mortis.

> *O Morning Star,*
> *splendour of light eternal and sun of*
> *righteousness:*
> *Come and enlighten those who dwell in*
> *darkness and the shadow of death.*

O Oriens

E vidi lume in forme de riviera   PARADISO XXX; 61

First light and then first lines along the east
To touch and brush a sheen of light on water
As though behind the sky itself they traced

The shift and shimmer of another river
Flowing unbidden from its hidden source;
The Day-Spring, the eternal Prima Vera.

Blake saw it too. Dante and Beatrice
Are bathing in it now, away upstream . . .
So every trace of light begins a grace

In me, a beckoning. The smallest gleam
Is somehow a beginning and a calling:
"Sleeper awake, the darkness was a dream

For you will see the Dayspring at your waking,
Beyond your long last line the dawn is breaking."

O Rex Gentium, et desideratus earum,
lapisque angularis, qui facis utraque unum:
veni, et salva hominem,
quem de limo formasti.

> *O King of the nations, and their desire,*
> *the cornerstone making both one:*
> *Come and save the human race,*
> *which you fashioned from clay.*

O Rex Gentium

O King of our desire whom we despise,
King of the nations never on the throne,
Unfound foundation, cast-off cornerstone,
Rejected joiner, making many one,
You have no form or beauty for our eyes,
A King who comes to give away his crown,
A King within our rags of flesh and bone.
We pierce the flesh that pierces our disguise,
For we ourselves are found in you alone.
Come to us now and find in us your throne,
O King within the child within the clay,
O hidden King who shapes us in the play
Of all creation. Shape us for the day
Your coming Kingdom comes into its own.

O Emmanuel, Rex et legifer noster,
exspectatio Gentium, et Salvator earum:
veni ad salvandum nos, Domine, Deus noster.

> *O Emmanuel, our king and our lawgiver,*
> *the hope of the nations and their Saviour:*
> *Come and save us, O Lord our God.*

O Emmanuel

O come, O come, and be our God-with-us
O long-sought With-ness for a world without,
O secret seed, O hidden spring of light.
Come to us Wisdom, come unspoken Name,
Come Root, and Key, and King, and holy Flame.
O quickened little wick so tightly curled,
Be folded with us into time and place,
Unfold for us the mystery of grace
And make a womb of all this wounded world.
O heart of heaven beating in the earth,
O tiny hope within our hopelessness
Come to be born, to bear us to our birth,
To touch a dying world with new-made hands
And make these rags of time our swaddling bands.

LINDA HEUMAN

Whose Buddhism Is Truest?

FROM *Tricycle*

TWO THOUSAND YEARS AGO, BUDDHIST MONKS ROLLED UP sutras written on birch bark, stuffed them into earthen pots, and buried them in a desert. We don't know why. They might have been disposing of sacred trash. Maybe they were consecrating a stupa. If they meant to leave a gift for future members of the Buddhist community—a wisdom time capsule, so to speak—they succeeded; and they could never have imagined how great that gift would turn out to be.

Fragments of those manuscripts, recently surfaced, are today stoking a revolution in scholars' understanding of early Buddhist history, shattering false premises that have shaped Buddhism's development for millennia and undermining the historical bases for Buddhist sectarianism. As the implications of these findings ripple out from academia into the Buddhist community, they may well blow away outdated, parochial barriers between traditions and help bring Buddhism into line with the pluralistic climate of our times.

Sometime probably around 1994, looters unearthed 29 birch bark scrolls somewhere in eastern Afghanistan or northwest Pakistan, an area once known as Gandhara—a Buddhist cultural hot spot during the early Christian era. The scrolls appeared on the antiquities market in Peshawar, having weathered the same turbulent political climate that would lead to the Taliban's demolition of the Bamiyan Buddhas. The British Library acquired them in 1994.

The scrolls arrived rolled up, flattened, folded, and disintegrating. Curators carefully unpacked and examined them. They found the script indecipherable, the language unusual. Suspecting that they might in fact be written in the forgotten language of Gandhari, they immediately sent a photograph to Richard Salomon, a professor of Sanskrit and Buddhist studies at the University of Washington, one of a handful of early Buddhist language experts worldwide who could read Gandhari.

The news soon came that the birch bark scrolls were the oldest Buddhist manuscripts known. (Now called the British Library Collection, these scrolls are in the process of being translated by the Early Buddhist Manuscript Project, a team of scholars under Salomon's direction.) The initial find was followed by several others throughout the following decade. Today there are at least five collections worldwide, comprising roughly a hundred texts and several hundred text fragments dating from the first century B.C.E. to the third century C.E. The Gandharan collections are not only the oldest extant Buddhist manuscripts but also the oldest surviving manuscripts of South Asia, period. They reach back into an era when the oral tradition of Buddhism probably first began to be written down.

Preliminary inventories and initial translations reveal that many texts are Gandhari versions of previously known Buddhist material, but most are new—including never-before-seen Abhidharma (Buddhist philosophy) treatises and commentaries, and stories set in contemporary Gandhara. The collections contain the earliest known Prajnaparamita (Perfection of Wisdom) texts and the earliest textual references to the Mahayana school, both

first century C.E. Taken together, these scrolls and scroll frag-
ments are a stunning find: an entirely new strand of Buddhist
literature.

According to experts in Gandhari, the new material is un-
likely to reveal earth-shattering facts about the Buddha. And don't
expect big surprises in terms of new doctrine either—no fifth
noble truth is likely to be found. But the discovery of a new mem-
ber in the Buddhist canonical family has profound implications
for practitioners. It settles the principal justification for long-
standing sibling rivalries among Buddhist traditions, and it does
so not by revealing a winner but by upending the cornerstone—
a false paradigm of history—on which such rivalries are based.

Buddhist tradition maintains that after his awakening, the
Buddha taught for some 45 years throughout eastern India. Among
his disciples were a few, including his attendant Ananda, who had
highly trained memories and could repeat his words verbatim. It is
said that after the Buddha's death, his disciples gathered at what
we now call the First Council, and these memorizers recited what
they had heard. Then all the monks repeated it, and the single and
definitive record of the "words of the Buddha" [*buddhavacana*] was
established. Thus was the Buddhist canon born.

Or was it?

Every school of Buddhism stakes its authority, and indeed its
very identity, on its historical connection to this original first
canon. Buddhists of all traditions have imagined that our texts
tumble from the First Council into our own hands whole and
complete—pristine—unshaped by human agency in their jour-
ney through time. This sense of the past is deeply ingrained and
compelling. If our texts don't faithfully preserve the actual words
of the Buddha in this way, we might think, how could they be
reliable? Isn't that what we base our faith on?

But as we're about to see, history works otherwise. And

having a view more in line with the facts here frees us from chauvinist views and gives us grounds for respecting differences between and within diverse Buddhist schools. As for undermining our basis for faith, not to worry. To get in line with the facts, we're not going to abandon Manjushri's sword of wisdom. We're going to use it.

I first heard about the Gandharan manuscripts while living in Germany in 2009, when I attended a lecture on early Buddhism by Professor Salomon, who was visiting from Seattle. The complex details of the talk he delivered left me mystified—at that point the technicalities of early Indian philology stood as a dense forest I hadn't yet entered. But I was curious about those scrolls. I wanted to understand what this new literary tradition meant for Buddhist practitioners like me.

While searching online, I found a 2006 talk by Salomon in which he first unveiled for a general audience the importance of translators' findings. Toward the end of that talk, my attention became riveted. As Salomon was explaining, scholars had traditionally expected that if they traced the various branches of the tree of Buddhist textual history back far enough, they would arrive at the single ancestral root. To illustrate this model, he pointed to a chart projected on the screen behind him. The chart showed the Gandhari canon as the potential missing link along an evolutionary ladder—the hypothetical antecedent of all other Buddhist canons. "This is how someone who began to study this [Gandharan] material might have thought the pattern worked."

As scholars scrutinized the Gandhari texts, however, they saw that history didn't work that way at all, Salomon said. It was a mistake to assume that the foundation of Buddhist textual tradition was singular, that if you followed the genealogical branches back far enough into the past they would eventually converge.

Traced back in time, the genealogical branches diverged and intertwined in such complex relationships that the model of a tree broke down completely. The picture looked more like a tangled bush, he reported.

Here is where I clicked Rewind: these newly found manuscripts, he declared, strike the *coup de grâce* to a traditional conception of Buddhism's past that has been disintegrating for decades. It is now clear that *none* of the existing Buddhist collections of early Indian scriptures—not the Pali, Sanskrit, Chinese, nor even the Gandhari—"can be privileged as the most authentic or original words of the Buddha."

It is odd how matters enacted on the wide stage of history can sometimes present themselves immediately in the close corners of personal life. I am a Mahayana practitioner; my partner practices in the Theravada tradition. The challenge of accommodating differences in the Buddhist family is an occasional cloud that hovers over our dinner table. What Salomon was saying seemed to indicate a new way of viewing and working with sectarian clashes at whatever level they might occur.

Puzzling out whether (and how) the discovery of a new Buddhist literary tradition could undermine sectarian sparring would lead me deep into the foreign terrain of academic Buddhism. In the months to come, I would follow a trail from one expert to another across college campuses from Seattle to Palo Alto. I pored over stacks of papers looking for insights. In the end, when it all came clear, I understood why the process had been so difficult. I had to assimilate new facts. I had to let go of some cherished beliefs. But what really made it hard was that also I had to identify and change a fundamental background picture I had about the nature of Buddhist history within which I construed those beliefs and assimilated those facts. I had to cut down the genealogical tree. And that was not easy, because I was sitting in it.

Actually, it isn't just historians of Buddhism who are find-
ing flaws in convergence-to-a-single-root pictures of the past. The
evolutionary tree model of origins is also under the axe in biology
and other scholastic fields. For some time there has been a broad
trend of thinking away from tree models of history, Salomon later
told me. In the academic study of early Buddhist history, Salo-
mon says, this model was gradually being discredited. But, he
says, these scrolls were "the clincher."

Because early Buddhism was an oral tradition, tracking any Bud-
dhist text back in time is like following a trail of bread crumbs
that ends abruptly. So for us looking to the past, a critical mo-
ment in history occurred when Buddhists started writing down
their texts rather than transmitting them orally. That is when the
Buddha's words moved into a more enduring form.

Pali tradition reports that Buddhist monks in the Theravada
tradition started writing down texts in about the first century
B.C.E. The manuscript record in Pali, however, doesn't begin until
about 800 C.E. But the Gandhari manuscripts date from as early
as the first century B.C.E. If monks were writing in one part of
India, they could likely have been writing in other parts of India
as well—so this would seem to add credence to the Pali claims.

If we were looking for a single ancestral root of all Buddhist
canons, the moment the teachings got written down would be
the first possible point in time we could find their physical record.
So when these Gandhari scrolls appeared, dating to the earliest
written era of Buddhism, scholars hoped they might turn out to
be that missing link. They zeroed in on the Gandhari literature
that had known versions in Pali, Sanskrit, and Chinese to see how
texts preserved in Gandhari related to other early Buddhist texts.
Comparing individual texts across canons, they noticed some-

thing startling and surprising, "although in retrospect," Salomon admitted in his lecture, "it should have been expected, and it makes perfect sense."

Salomon described what happened when he compared the Gandhari version of one well-known Buddhist poem, the *Rhinoceros Sutra*, to its Pali and Sanskrit versions. He found that the sequence of verses and their arrangement were similar to the Pali. The specific wording of the poem, however, was much closer to the Sanskrit. Salomon couldn't say whether the Gandhari was more closely related to one or the other version (as it would have to be if one were the parent). It was closely related to both, but in different ways. In other words, the texts were parallel—and different.

This kind of complex linking showed up again and again when scholars compared Gandhari texts with their versions in Pali, Sanskrit, and Chinese. Texts had close parallels to one, two, and sometimes all three of the other language versions. Looking then at the group as a whole, they ascertained that this new corpus of Gandhari material was a parallel to, and not an antecedent of, the other canons—not the missing parent, but a long-lost sibling.

We now know that if there ever was a point of convergence in the Buddhist family tree—the missing link, the single original and authentic Buddhist canon—it is physically lost in the era of oral transmission. We have not yet found, and probably will not ever find, evidence for it.

But even more significant is what we *have* found: that is, difference. These scrolls are incontrovertible proof that as early as the first century B.C.E., there was another significant living Buddhist tradition in a separate region of India and in an entirely different language from the tradition preserved in Pali.

"And where there are two, we are now on very solid ground in suggesting there were many more than two," says Collett Cox, a professor of Sanskrit and Buddhist studies at the University of Washington and the co-director of the Early Buddhist Manuscript Project. A single partial Gandhari Buddhist manuscript predated these modern finds—a version of the *Dharmapada* discovered in 1892. The fact of one extant manuscript in the Gandhari language suggested, but couldn't prove, that Gandhara had once had a rich literary tradition. In the same way, there are other indicators— such as monuments and inscriptions—in other parts of India suggesting other potentially literate early Buddhist cultures. "We don't have any texts from them," Cox says. "But we now are on very solid ground in saying they probably had texts too. Where there are two [traditions], there are probably five. And where there are five, there may have been fifteen or twenty-five."

Cox suggests that "rather than asking the question what single language did the Buddha use and what represents the earliest version of his teachings, we might have to accept that from the very beginning there were various accounts of his teachings, different sutras, and different versions of sutras transmitted in different areas. At the very beginning we might have a number of different sources, all of whom represent or claim to represent the teaching of the Buddha." Cox emphasizes that the Gandharan Buddhism is clearly not a "rebel offshoot" of the Pali canon but its own entirely localized strand—unique, but not unrelated. Early Buddhists in different regions shared many texts in common. Clearly, Buddhist monks of different language traditions in early India were in contact, and they traded ideas and influenced each other in complex ways.

If a multiplicity of traditions is what we have now, and as far as the record goes back in time, multiplicity is what we've always had, maybe we're not finding a single root of Buddhism because there wasn't one in the first place. Sometimes not-finding is, after all, the supreme finding.

. . .

"Nobody holds the view of an original canon anymore," Oskar von Hinüber, one of the world's leading scholars of Pali, told me.

Consider why scholars might think this. First of all, there are certain practical difficulties of oral transmission in a time before digital recording. How could 500 monks have agreed on 45 years of the Buddha's words?

Von Hinüber also points out that the sutras themselves record a deep and persistent quarrel between the Buddha's attendant, Ananda, and Mahakasyapa, who presided over the Council and was the principal disciple at the time of the Buddha's death. He suggests that it would be Pollyannaish to imagine that the Council (if it even occurred) was politic-free and harmonious.

"There are many indications that [the stories of the First Council] are not correct in the way of a historical report. But they tell us something that is interesting and important," says von Hinüber. "Buddhists themselves were aware of the fact that at some point in history their texts must have been shaped by somebody into the standard form they now have, beginning *Thus have I heard*. Who this was, we don't know."

Interestingly, built into the traditional account of the First Council is the story of one monk who arrived late. He asked the others what he had missed. When they told him how they had formalized the Buddha's teachings, he objected. He insisted that he himself had heard the Buddha's discourses and would continue to remember them as he had heard them.

"This is a very important story," says von Hinüber, "because it shows that Buddhists themselves were aware of the fact of diverging traditions."

Religious orthodoxy wants to claim that one's own tradition is the best. To do that, one needs to point to something unique to make it so. Having the sole true version of a singular truth is just such a foothold. And not only for Buddhists. Elaine Pagels, the scholar of religion who brought to light the Gnostic gospels, told *Tricycle* in 2005:

> The Church father Tertullian said, *Christ taught one single thing, and that's what we teach, and that is what is in the creed.* But he's writing this in the year 180 in North Africa, and what he says Christ taught would never fit in the mouth of a rabbi, such as Jesus, in first-century Judea. For a historically based tradition—like Christianity, and as you say, Buddhism—there's a huge stake in the claim that what it teaches goes back to a specific revelation, person, or event, and there is a strong tendency to deny the reality of constant innovation, choice, and change.

The Buddhist canons as they exist today are the products of historical contingencies. They resound with the many voices that have shaped them through time. But orthodoxy requires the opposite, a wall you can't put your fist through: singular, unchanging, findable truth. Buddhism's textual root wasn't singular, and it wasn't unchanging. As it turns out, it wasn't so findable, either.

"That's the further step that we're taking, to dispense with the idea of the original because that is a kind of pipe dream or figment of the imagination," says Paul Harrison, a professor of religious studies at Stanford University and a member of the editorial board for the Schøyen Collection (another recently discovered collection of ancient Buddhist manuscripts). Harrison is also a translator. As such, he gives us a hands-on report of how texts weather the practicalities of translation. To the extent that we are still holding on to that tree model, Harrison is about to pull the last leaves from our hands. Translators used to be guided by the notion, he explains, that if you put enough different versions of a sutra together, kept the overlap, and eliminated all the variance, eventually you could reconstruct the prototype. "According to that model," he says, "it'll all narrow to a point. But basically what we are finding is that it doesn't narrow to a point. The more we know, the more varied and indeterminate it is right at the beginning." Trying to reconstruct the original version of any early sutra—the one that is unmediated, accurate, and complete—is now generally considered, in principle, futile. Indeed, Harrison asks, "What are you aiming at?" Looking for such an original is ingrained, essentialist thinking, he says.

He points out, "We often say, 'Tibetan translation, Chinese translation, *Sanskrit original*. As soon as you say *Sanskrit original*, you drop back into that sloppy but entirely natural way of thinking, that this is the original so we can throw away the copies. But in fact, that Sanskrit original of whatever sutra is just again another version. So the idea that one of them is the original and all the others are more or less imperfect shadows of it has to be given up. But it is very hard to give it up. It's almost impossible to give it up." And the irony is not lost on Harrison, who adds. "This is what the teaching of the Buddha is all about."

One problem with the traditional model of textual transmission, according to Harrison, is that it doesn't take into account cross-influences—the very real cases of text conflation when scribes or translators might have (for example, when standardizing) copied features from multiple differing versions, thus producing a new version. He continues: "If everything just proceeds in its own vertical line, and there is no crossways influence, that is fine; you know where you are. But once things start flowing horizontally, you get a real mess. Having something old, of course, is valuable because you are more likely to be closer to an earlier form. But notice I'm careful to say now '*an* earlier form' and not '*the* earliest form.' A first-century B.C.E. [Gandhari] manuscript is going to give you a better guide to an earlier form than an 18th-century Sri Lankan copy will. But that's not an absolute guarantee, just a slightly better one."

Harrison says that not only is it *physically* unlikely that we could find an original Buddhist canon (because the teachings predated writing), but also it is *theoretically impossible*, according to the Buddha's own teachings on the nature of reality. "It is pure *anatmavada* [the doctrine of nonself, non-essentialism]. We expect it [the original *buddhavacana*] to be the same—invariable and unchanging, kind of crisp and sharp at the sides all around."

That is, after all, the kind of canon that Buddhists who make historical claims to authenticity—and all Buddhist schools have traditionally made such claims and based their authority on them—believe their tradition possesses or other traditions lack: not a "one-of-many-versions" canon but "the real one."

"It's just not going to be like that," Harrison says.

What would it mean to have "all the Buddha's teachings"? Would it be every word he said? What about meaningful silences? Well, would it be what he meant then? When he said what to whom? About what? We can't pin down the complete content of the Buddha's teachings, nor can we isolate the teachings from their context. We can't draw a hard line around them.

Neither can we draw a solid line around different schools. Harrison reports that looking backward in time, already by the first century C.E. boundaries between the Mahayana and non-Mahayana begin to blur. The Gandhari manuscripts probably reflect content of early monastic libraries, and the texts seem to have been intentionally buried. Mahayana and mainstream Buddhist sutras were recovered together and presumably buried together. Harrison believes that the monks who engaged in Mahayana practices were most likely Vinaya-observing; they likely lived in monasteries side by side practitioners of more mainstream Buddhism.

These first-century Mahayana texts in the new collections are already highly developed in terms of narrative complexity and Mahayana doctrine. They couldn't be the first Mahayana sutras, · Harrison says. "The earlier stages of the Mahayana go *far* back. The Mahayana has longer roots and older roots than we thought before." (Not roots all the way back to the Buddha, though—Harrison agrees with the general scholarly consensus that the Mahayana developed after the Buddha.) Nonetheless, he says, "Probably lying behind these Mahayana texts there are others with much stronger mainstream coloration, where it is not so easy to tell whether it's Mahayana or Shravakayana." (Shravakayana means literally "the way of the hearers"; those who follow the path with arahantship as its goal.)

During this period of early Buddhism, there were many different strands of practice and trends of thought that were not yet linked. "We could have the Perfection of Wisdom strand and a Pure Land strand and a worship of the Buddha strand, and all sorts of things going on," Harrison remarks. Only later did these threads coalesce into what we now consider "the Mahayana."

Harrison suggested we consider a braided river as a better metaphor than a tree for the historical development of Buddhist traditions. A braided river has a number of strands that fan out and reunite. "Its origin is not one spring, but a marsh or a network of small feeder streams," he told me. According to this model, the Mahayana and Vajrayana "are merely downstream in the onward flow of creativity. They are activities similar in nature to early Buddhism—not radically different. And a lot of current in their channels has come all the way from the headwaters," he says. "Whether it all has the single taste of liberation is another question."

In such a picture of textual transmission—fluid, dynamic, and intermingled—where and how could one stake a territorial claim? Sectarian posturing is based on having *the* actual words of the Buddha—complete, stable, unmediated, and self-contained. Once all one can have is a *complex of versions* of the Buddha's words—partial, changing, shaped, and commingled with other versions—in what sense would it be *authoritative* if one's own version was bottled upstream or down?

But I still wanted to drink my water bottled upstream even though I knew that kind of thinking no longer made sense. I couldn't put my finger on what was bothering me. Finally, I looked inside my glass. What did I assume was in it? What do we imagine we have when we have the Buddha's words?

We think that if we have the Buddha's actual words we have his true intent. The whole edifice of sectarian claims based on history remained teetering on this.

Somehow we picture the Buddha's true, single, unambiguous meaning encapsulated in his words like jewels inside a box, passed from one generation to the next like Grandmother's heirlooms. But that's not the way meanings or words work. Consider the following from the well-known scholar of religion Robert Bellah:

> Zen Buddhism began in Japan at a time when strong social structures hemmed in individuals on every side. The family you were born to determined most of your life-chances. Buddhism was a way to step outside these constricting structures. Becoming a monk was called *shukke*, literally, "leaving the family." We live in an almost completely opposite kind of society, where all institutions are weak and the family is in shambles. You don't need Buddhism to "leave the family." To emphasize primarily the individualistic side of Buddhism (es-

pecially Zen) in America is only to contribute to our
pathology, not ameliorate it.

In India, "leaving the family" means "getting married." To
my Jewish grandmother, it meant "changing religions." In the
household where I was raised, it meant "going to college." The very
same words, spoken in a different context, have different mean-
ings. The meaning of words is their *use in context*. A set of words
stripped of their context is like playing pieces stripped of their
board game. What would we have?

Certainly it would be good to know what the Buddha said.
To the extent that we share the conventions of 5th-century B.C.E.
Indians, we might understand some of what he meant. If we in-
creased the conventions we shared with them (say, by learning
early Indian languages or by studying history), obviously we
would understand more. But context is vast—an unbounded, in-
terdependent web of connections. And it is dynamic, shifting
moment to moment. Context is finished the moment it happens;
then it is a new context. We really can't recreate it. And even if we
could, we still wouldn't know exactly how the Buddha was *using*
his words within that context, so we wouldn't know exactly what
he *meant*.

Just as our search for an original set of Buddha's definitive
words failed, and all we were left with were provisional versions,
in the same way a search for the Buddha's definitive meaning fails
too. What we have are traditions of interpretation. But that's not
the kind of authority we imagine when we claim sectarian pri-
macy. Sectarian authority claims assume solid essentialist ground.
That type of ground is just not there.

When it comes right down to it, sectarian posturing contradicts
the Buddha's message as all traditions understand it. Those false

pictures of history and language within which sectarianism finds a foothold are in turn rooted in another false picture—a picture even more pervasive and pernicious. That picture is an essentialist view of the nature of reality, which according to the Buddha's doctrine of selflessness is the source of not just this but *all* our suffering—the wrong view that is *the very point of Buddhism* to refute.

The siblings in my family don't have a single, same, enduring, essential feature in common that connects us to each other (or to our ancestors), nor do we need one. Anyone could pick us out of a crowd as related. I have my father's nose and my aunt's height; my sister has my grandmother's hair and my father's fast walk; my brother looks like my father and me. The traditions of the Buddhist family can dress, think, and practice differently and still be recognizable family members in exactly the same way in which the members of our own family are recognizably related to us.

All the siblings in my family are authentic members of my family. Because our identity doesn't depend on our possessing some unchanging "common thing," we don't have to argue over who has more of it. If we understand identity in this way, all Buddhists are 100 percent Buddhist.

Letting go of our old assumptions about history and language shouldn't make us uneasy. The views we're challenging as we assimilate these new archaeological discoveries were never Buddhist to begin with. We're not abandoning the basis for our faith; we're confirming it. And in so doing, we open up the possibility to truly appreciate different Buddhist traditions as equal members of our Buddhist family.

Forgiveness

FROM *Agni*

IT HAPPENED IN ISTANBUL, ON THE TRAM RUNNING BETWEEN Eminonu and Sultanahmet, one August night at about eleven. I'd been in the city for a few weeks, working with Turkish teachers of English, and was returning from dinner with my new friend, Gulayse, a novelist. We'd talked late at Hamdi's, a restaurant near the spice market. Afterward she'd walked me to the tram stop at Eminonu. A bell clanged, the tram slid into the station, and the doors opened smoothly. Then they shut behind me, sealing the crowded car.

Three men stood facing the door. We looked at each other. "American?" the one closest to me asked. He was wearing a cotton shirt, short-sleeved, with stripes across the chest. His mouth was fixed in a little smile, his teeth faintly stained with nicotine. "American." I nodded. "And you?" "Iraqi," he said, looking at me closely. We were almost touching. "American kill Iraqi," he said.

His face swam up in front of mine. "Terrible—" I said, looking down. His answer came swiftly. "No you," he said. He spoke rapidly and I understood only a little. "Baby," he said and with his arm made a motion of someone throwing something away. "Baby." Again he flung his arm sideways. His face was inches from mine, his eyes rimmed with red. "I am so sorry," I said. He watched me, his mouth still fixed in a little smile. Then: "It's improve now. American leaving."

Only nights before, I'd been sitting in a small café on the Hippodrome across from the Blue Mosque. It was the night of the full moon and I could make out the hieroglyphs on the Egyptian obelisk, the stalking bird at the top. After a while the final call to prayer poured into the square, the voice of the muezzin gliding from note to half-note. The call continued a long time, it seemed, longer than usual. "What's happening?" I asked the waiter.

"This is one of the holiest nights of the year," he said. "Tonight all Muslims ask forgiveness for the harm they know they've done. For the harm they don't know too. Ask forgiveness for their daughters and sons, for parents who are dead. For everyone."

I followed the sidewalk along the edge of the Hippodrome to the mosque, entered the enormous court crowded with people, some taking off their shoes to enter, some washing at spigots in the great fountain, others sitting praying in the side galleries, men and women, many children, too, moving between. The white moon behind the minarets appeared enormous. Seagulls, as always, drifted back and forth. When I walked out into the Hippodrome again, I noticed what I hadn't before: that cars solidly filled the sidewalks, that people were sitting silently on the grass, hands lifted.

The waiter was still standing at the edge of his café. I told him I'd just been to the mosque. "I hope you do not take offense," he replied, "but I pray for you too."

EDWARD HIRSCH

The Custodian

FROM *The Atlantic*

Sometimes I think I have lived
My whole life like that old janitor
Who locked up after the rabbi
And patrolled the synagogue at night.

He never learned the Hebrew prayers,
Which he hummed under his breath
As he folded the soiled tallises
And stacked the skullcaps into piles.

He opened the Holy Ark by hand
And dusted off the sacred scrolls,
O Lord, which he never opened,
And cut the light behind the organ.

He ignored the Eternal Lamp
(Woe to the worker who unplugged it!),
As he vacuumed the House of Prayer
Muddied by the congregation.

Not for him the heavenly choir music
Or the bearded sermon handed down

From the lectern, though stars squinted
Through the stained-glass windows.

Every now and then he'd sigh
And stare up at the domed ceiling
As if he had heard something auspicious,
But it was only the wind in the trees.

He picked a prayer book off the floor
And carried it down to the basement,
Where he chewed on a sandwich
And listened to a ballgame on the radio.

JANE HIRSHFIELD

In Daylight, I Turned On the Lights

FROM *The New Yorker*

In daylight, I turned on the lights,
in darkness, I pulled closed the curtains.
And the god of *More*,
whom nothing surprises, softly agreed—
each day, year after year,
the dead were dead one day more completely.
In the places where morels were found,
I looked for morels.
In the house where love was found,
I looked for love.
If she vanished, what then was different?
If he is alive, what now is changed?
The pot offers the metal closest to fire for burning.
The water leaves.

EDWARD HOAGLAND

When I Was Blind

FROM *Portland*

I WAS BLIND FOR A WHILE, AND WALKING IN THE WOODS WAS AN adventure. The white bark of birch trees beckoned to me. I would stroll through cushiony dead poplar leaves or fountaining ferns like ostrich plumes as high as my chest. I could hear squirrels quarreling and veerys veerying. Wood sorrel grew underfoot, the leaves tart when you taste them. Bears fattened on beechnuts in the fall up here and pitcher plants and orchids could be found in a kind of suspended bog.

When I was blind I listened to the radio scanner chatter softly, pulling in transmissions from the State Police, the Sheriff's Department, the Border Patrol, the town Rescue Squad, and the hospital at the county seat. You could also hear several fire departments, the Fish and Game frequency that wardens called in on, the Civil Air Patrol, railroad dispatchers, and various ham channels that lonely civilians talked on. You might hear EMT personnel resuscitate a heart patient, panting over him on air; or a fire in progress, actually even crackling; or a cop chasing a car thief through the woods, but mostly highway crews gabbing with headquarters interminably.

. . .

My neighbor trapped fisher, fox, and beaver in the swamp in season, shot venison, caught catfish, logged pulpwood, knew where the otters denned and the herons nested, where snappers could be dug out for a turtle stew, where a patch of lady's-slippers flourished where any girl might pick a moccasin-flower for her prom. But he had medical bills, and no money laid aside till his social security kicked in, so he was a junkyard watchman for money. The man who owned the junkyard was a war veteran too and both men knew the old bootlegger paths through the swamp. The swamp was eight miles wide, and you could make a living limbing cedar trees and dragging them out for post-and-rail fencing or patio furniture, or from saw-log cherry wood or yellow birch and bird's-eye maple in the higher spots. Japanese businessmen owned the swamp now, having bought it from Wall Street investors, who had bought it from the logging company who had worked it over when everybody was young. The logging company had employed the county's jailbirds to cut tamaracks for telephone poles, plus any local who wanted to slug it out with the trees, hauling with horses as often as not, because of the braided streams. It was a good life until you broke a leg or got a rupture, and the logging led you into necks of the woods where nobody had trapped lately and you might nab a sixty-dollar bobcat overnight, half a month's pay.

When you are blind you can hear people smile—there's a soft click when their lips part. Once I went to see a healer in the woods. "Ease up on milk and Tums. Are you centered with the Lord? Do you tithe? Are you asking Him for guidance? Is your daughter in trouble? I have patients who fall out of bed every night, their dreams are so bad. Smoke much? Lemme see your nails. Chew your nails? You pray? Farm paid for? Be tremulous before the Lord! I'll pray for you, if you wish. But you wouldn't want me spitting into your eyes, like Jesus did with the blind man. Am I right? Praise the Lord. Eat less. Unquietness eats at you. Stand underneath God. Get under His spotlight. No charge."

It used to be that the way you milked cows was you strapped a milking stool to your butt and wore it like a stiff set of bug's legs sticking out for half the day. No more. In the old days here, before the economics of farming forced you to trundle each cow off to be ground into hamburger once her most productive years were past, you'd become friends with your cows, and you felt an intimacy with the personalities of each, milking by hand, not machine. Although you shot every hawk or owl you saw, you treated your cows better then.

When I was blind I loved to ride trains, to sit in the Observation Car and chat with strangers, or in the dining car, the club car. When you can't see, age is less of a factor, no skin tone or paunchy posture to go by. Voices wrinkle later than faces, and, emanating from inside, seem truer to the nature residing there, harder to educate in concealment or deceit. Voices register compassion, disdain, apprehension, confidence, or surprise more directly, if you've learned to listen.

Rain squalls wet the spiders' webs just enough to glisten so that I could see them, though trees remained a bit of a puzzle, like shapes viewed underwater. But I could hear better—the giggle of the flying loons, rattle of a kingfisher, a hermit thrush seeking an answer from distant softwoods, the passage of a large milk snake through the stone wall where it ate chipmunks.

Another neighbor, who worked at the sawmill, had taught his dog to snatch food scraps out of the air when he, the neighbor, was having lunch and tossed them. But one day two of his fingers were sliced off by the saw and flew through the air and the dog caught and ate them. So I'm a part of him now for as long as he lives, said the guy.

When your sight evaporates, your forehead seems to lower incrementally, appropriating the area formerly occupied by the eyes. Thus more brain space is created—as well as more time to think. You hope.

Offered for auction today in town: cows, a llama, a guitar, a hare, a truck tire, a wheelchair. Who died? Play it safe, says the auctioneer, you'll never get one cheaper when you need it. Afterwards the cashier puts a bottle of whiskey on the counter, signaling the end of the auction and a drink for everyone with money for a poker game.

Blindness was full of second sight. I saw how the money economy had failed my neighbors after a lifetime of busy days, a web of energetic routines. Their house insurance had lapsed, the property tax bill was a yearly ordeal, but social security hadn't yet kicked in. So fragile, though surges of mercy in other people did bubble up.

PICO IYER

Maximum India

FROM *Condé Nast Traveler*

THERE WERE FIRES, SIX, SEVEN OF THEM, RISING THROUGH THE winter fog. Groups of men, scarves wrapped around their heads, eyes blazing in the twilight, were gathered barefoot around the flames, edging closer. A near-naked man with dusty, matted dreadlocks down to his waist was poking at a charred head with a bamboo pole. There was chanting in the distance, a shaking of bells, a furious, possessed drumming, and in the infernal no-light of the winter dusk, I could make out almost nothing but orange blazes, far off, by the river.

How much of this was I dreaming? How much was I under a "foreign influence," if only of jet lag and displacement? Figures came toward me out of the mist, smeared in ash from head to toe, bearing the three-pronged trident of the city's patron, Shiva, the Ender of Time. In the little alleyways behind the flames was a warren of tiny streets; a shrunken candle burned in the dark of a bare earth cavern where men were whispering sacred syllables. Cows padded ceaselessly down the clogged, dung-splattered lanes, and every now and then another group of chanters surged past me, a dead body under a golden shroud on the bamboo stretcher that they carried toward the river, and I pressed myself against a wall as the whisper of mortality brushed past.

It was hard to believe that, just three days before, I had been in California, marking a quiet New Year's Day in the sun. Now there were goats with auspicious red marks on their foreheads trotting around, and embers burning, and oil lamps drifting out across the river in the fog. Along the walls beside the river were painted faces, laughing monkey gods, sacred looming phalluses. The shops on every side were selling sandalwood paste, and clarified butter oil for dead bodies, and tiny clay urns for their ashes.

Imagine finding yourself in a Hare Krishna celebration as populous as Philadelphia. All around you, people are shaking bells, whirling, singing joyfully, though their joy has to do with death, as if everything is upended in a holy universe. At the nearby Manikarnika Well, the god Shiva is said to have met the god Vishnu, usually an occupant of a parallel world. The result of this propitious encounter is that bodies are burned in public there—as many as a hundred a day—and the most sacred spot in the center of Hinduism is a smoking charnel-ground.

On paper, Varanasi is a holy crossroads, a place of transformation tucked between the Varana and Asi rivers, along the sacred Ganges. It is, many will tell you, the oldest continuously inhabited city on earth, as ancient as Babylon or Thebes. Because the city, now housing as many as three million (half a million of them squeezed into the square mile of the Old City), has never been a center of political power or historical conflict, it has been able to continue undisturbed, and fundamentally unchanged, as the most sacred citadel of Hinduism and a cultural hot spot. Bathe yourself in its filthy waters, devout Hindus believe, and you purify yourself for life. Die or be burned along its banks and you achieve *moksha*, or liberation, from the cycle of incarnation.

But if Varanasi means anything, it is the explosion of every theory and the turning of paper to ash. The heart of the city is a chaotic three-mile stretch of waterfront along Mother Ganga on which there are more than seventy ghats, or steps, from which the faithful can walk down into the water. At the top of these steps stand huge, many-windowed palaces and temples that are all in a state of such advanced decay that they seem to speak for the impermanence of everything. At this very spot, the southeast-flowing Ganges turns, briefly, so it seems to be flowing back toward the Himalayas from which it came, and bathers on its western bank can face the rising sun. Varanasi's original name, Kashi, means City of Light, although millennia of dusty rites and blazing bodies and holy men showing no interest in normal human laws have also left it a city of shadows or, as the wonderfully obsessive Varanasiphile Richard Lannoy writes, a "city of darkness and dream."

The son of Indian-born parents, I am (in theory) a Hindu, and though I have never practiced the religion, I was finding Varanasi to be more a mad confusion than the sublime order that a good Hindu would see. Yet in the months before I made my first trip to the city, everywhere I turned seemed to lead there, as if by magnetic attraction. Writing on Buddhism, I was reminded that the Buddha delivered his first discourse at Sarnath, six miles from Varanasi. Meeting a professor of Sanskrit in California, I was told that Shankara, the great Hindu philosopher, had accepted his first disciple in Varanasi and was said to have met Shiva there, in the disguise of an untouchable, more than a thousand years ago. This was where Peter Matthiessen began his epic Himalayan quest, recorded in *The Snow Leopard*; this was where Allen Ginsberg was shadowed by local intelligence and confessed, of the city's residents, "They're all mad."

Varanasi seemed to mark the place where opposites were pushed together so intensely that all sense gave out. Its holy waters flow, for example, past thirty sewers, with the result that the brownish stuff the devout are drinking and bathing in contains three thousand times the maximum level of fecal coliform bacteria considered safe by the World Health Organization. Those old collapsing buildings along its banks, suggesting some immemorial pageant, are in fact not old at all, although they do confirm the sense that one has entered less a city than an allegory of some kind, a cosmogram legible only to a few. Everything is constantly shifting, flickering this way and that in the candlelit phantasmagoria, and yet the best description I found of twenty-first-century Varanasi—"There is movement, motion, human life everywhere, and brilliantly costumed"—was penned by Mark Twain in the nineteenth.

A city that is truly holy is as contrary and multidirectional as any charismatic human, and draws people almost regardless of their faith or origins. So perhaps I should not have been surprised that, the minute I landed following the fifty-minute flight from Delhi and set foot in Varanasi, which was shrouded in a miasmal early-January mist, I ran into a Tibetan incarnate lama, an American Tibetan Buddhist monk I know from New York, and a ninety-one-year-old Parisienne I'd last seen attending teachings of the Dalai Lama's in Dharamsala.

"Oh," she said, unsurprised, "you are here too."

The Dalai Lama, I gathered, was giving his only official teachings of the winter and spring in Sarnath, right there, that very week.

The living capital of Hinduism is home, too, to fourteen hundred mosques and shrines, and every religious teacher from Jiddu Krishnamurti to Thich Nhat Hanh has spent time here; it was here that Mohandas Gandhi entered Indian political life in 1916 (when, at the inauguration of the local Banaras Hindu University, he spoke out against the filth of the city's holy places), and it was here that the French explorer Alexandra David-Neel received lessons in yoga from a naked swami before heading to Tibet.

I got into a car and entered the swirling river of life that in Varanasi reflects and flows into its central symbol. India specializes in intensity and chaos—part of the governing logic of Varanasi is that it is crowded with traffic and yet there are no traffic lights—and very soon I was careening through the crush (a riot in search of a provocation, so it seemed): Here and there an elderly policeman with a mask over his mouth held out an arm, and cars, cows, bicycles, and trucks crashed past him, willy-nilly. Dogs were sleeping in the middle of a busy road—Varanasi's Fifth Avenue, it might have been—and men were outstretched (sleeping, I hoped) along the side and on the pavement. I dropped my bags at my hotel, The Gateway, and in the course of the twenty-minute ride to the river, I saw two more jubilant corpse processions and two parades of children—in honor, I could only imagine, of the God of Mayhem.

"This is a very inauspicious time," my guide warned me from the front seat. "It is called Kharamas. Everyone stays hidden; no one talks about weddings, things like that. Everyone is silent. It is like a curse placed on the city."

I could find no mention of any such observance, but if this was Varanasi at its most silent, I thought, I couldn't imagine it on one of its frequent festival days. "The curse lifts on January 14," my new friend told me. "Then we celebrate." This was not cause for celebration to someone due to depart, as I was, on January 13.

At a Christian church, we got out and joined the crush of bodies pushing toward the Ganges. We walked along the path to the riverbank, dodging the refuse and excrement of centuries, and passed an almost naked man, staring right at us, sheltered by a small fire inside a hut.

"He's meditating?" I tried.

"Everything for him is ashes," came the reply. Philosophy is ceaseless along the Ganges, and usually causeless. Holy men sat on the ground under umbrellas, chanting and smearing paste and ash on their foreheads. "These sadhus, they like very much to live with cremation. They don't wear clothes as we do. They don't do anything like people who are living in the material world. They want to live in a world of ash." To come here was like entering one of the narrow, winding old cities of Europe—my birthplace of Oxford, in fact—in which you are back in a medieval mix of high scholasticism and faith.

A huge, bloated cow floated past us, and we climbed into a boat as five handsome young boys in elaborate gold pantaloons held up five-armed oil lamps in a glossy fire ceremony along the river. Fires were blazing to the north and south, and the air was thick with the smell of incense and burning. "Only in this city, sir, you see twenty-four-hour cremation," offered the boatman, as if speaking of a convenience store. In other cities, cremation grounds are traditionally placed outside the city gates. Here, they burn at the center of all life.

The next day, a little before daybreak, I walked out of the gates of my hotel to visit the river again. Only one man was standing there now, under a tree, with a bicycle-rickshaw—his eyes afire in his very dark face, and what looked to be a bullet hole in his cheek. We negotiated for a while and then took off into the penumbral gloom, the previously jam-packed streets under a kind of sorcerer's spell, quite empty.

To travel by bicycle in the dawn is to feel all the sounds, smells, and ancient ghosts of Varanasi; for more than a week, the bicycle-rickshaw man would become my faithful friend, waiting outside the gates of the hotel, ready to guide me anywhere. The winter fog only compounded the half-dreamed air of the place, as figures loomed out of the clouds to stare at us, and then vanished abruptly, as if nothing was quite substantial here, or even true. *"Unreal City,"* I thought, remembering a boyhood ingestion of T. S. Eliot. *"Under the brown fog of a winter dawn . . . I had not thought death had undone so many."*

On the Ganges, a Charon pulled me soundlessly across the water, past all the broken palaces, the huge flights of steps, the men and women walking down to the water, barely clothed, dipping their heads in and shaking themselves dry, as if awakening from a long sleep. "In Varanasi," said the ferryman, "thirty-five, forty percent is holy men." In another boat, an Indian man with his young wife and child had his laptop open in the phantasmal dark. Cows, pariah dogs, and figures in blankets appeared in the mist, and red-bottomed monkeys ran in and out of the temples. "Sir," said the boatman, and I braced myself for an offer of young girls, young boys, or drugs. "You would like *darshan*? I arrange meeting with holy man for you?"

All this, of course, is the Varanasi of sightseers, the almost psyche-delic riddle at the eye of the storm that entices many, horrifies others, and leaves most feeling as if they are losing their mind. But part of the power of the holy city is that it is shaped very consciously—like a mandala, some say, a series of concentric sa-cred zones—and as you move away from the river, you come out into a world that is India's highest center of learning and re-finement, home to its greatest scholars for as long as anyone can remember.

"It is such a beautiful city," said Pramod Chandra, an elegant soul who comes from a long line of Varanasi thinkers and writers (and who is a professor emeritus of art at Harvard). We were seated in his large, bare family home not far from the burning ghats and the crumbling palaces. "If they did it up, it could be like one of the great cities of Spain or Italy. The tall houses in the

Old City? If you go inside, you find abundant worlds there—courtyards and inner spaces, everything. But the problem in India is always bureaucracy. It's deadening." There was now, he said, a plan for creating a futuristic overpass around the Old City, so as to turn the maze of ill-lit alleyways into a kind of inner suburb.

Because the buildings of Varanasi are only about 350 years old, the city has always had to sustain its traditions in human ways, through rites and ideas; it is not the stones or monuments that give Varanasi its sense of continuity, as in Jerusalem or at Kailas, but the unchanging customs passed down from father to son to grandson. The professor recalled for me, over a long evening of talk, the days when educated boys here learned Sanskrit from pandits who came to their homes, committing to memory huge swatches of holy text.

So part of the deeper fascination of the City of Light, beyond the visceral shock, is the way it brings together back-lane black magic and high-flown speculation and, in so doing, serves as India's India, a concentrated distillate of the culture's special mix of cloudy philosophizing and unembarrassed reality. Spirituality in Varanasi lies precisely in the poverty and sickness and death that it weaves into its unending tapestry; a place of holiness, it says, is not set apart from the world, in a Shangri-la of calm, but a place where purity and filth, anarchy and ritual, unquenchable vitality and the constant imminence of death all flow together.

In Varanasi, as everywhere in India, the first rule of survival is that getting anywhere at all—from A to B via T, Q, and Z—is an ordeal; but settling into some quiet corner and joining in the rhythm of life around you can make for one of the most cozy and companionable stays imaginable. The center of life is Asi Ghat, at the southern end of the line of ghats, which has now turned into a foreigner-friendly neighborhood of eco-institutes and Salsa

Dance Aerobics classes, pizza restaurants and compendious book-shops. And the epicenter of Asi Ghat, for the fortunate few, is the Hotel Ganges View, an unassuming-looking place whose thirteen rooms are usually filled with some of the most interesting Vara-nasi watchers you will ever meet.

Here you can find yourself sharing a table on a candlelit roof-top with a Danish psychiatrist working with trauma in Iraq, Rwanda, and Bosnia, and a German scholar of Hinduism. After dinner, the low-ceilinged dining room was turned into a back-drop for an intimate concert, and as I sat there, being whipped up into the ether by two sarangi players and a tabla virtuoso, a gnom-ish man with tufts of white hair and a tweed jacket came in. He looked back at me and casually nodded, and I realized that it was a German singer of Sufi *ghazals* whom I had last seen in the Tier-garten in Berlin, talking of Ethiopia and Mali.

Varanasi has at times this feeling of being an insider's secret, marked on the invisible map that certain initiates carry around with them, and as the days went on, I came to see that the con-stant back-and-forth—the advance into the intensities of the river, the retreat to a place from which to contemplate them all—was part of the natural rhythm of the city. Every time I stepped out of my hotel to be greeted by my loyal friend with his rickshaw, I was pitched into the Boschian madness of a teeming, pell-mell cacophony in which, amid the constant plodding of beasts, I saw ads for an Institute of Call Centre Training, notices for "radio jockey certificate courses," signs for those dreaming to become "air stewardesses." The promise of the new India is that even the poorest kid in the slums, if he applies himself at a Brain Gym, can make it not to the NBA but to an MBA course, and to the once-unimaginable world marked out by the shining new malls and ubiquitous signs for McVeggie with Cheese. Such is the inclusiveness of Varanasi and the hundreds of gods it houses that the new is taken in as readily as the old.

We would clatter through the mob and arrive at the river, and I would be reminded how and why members of my own (Hindu, India-dwelling) family would often tell me. "Don't go to Benares [as Varanasi was long known]! It's just stench and crooks and dirt. Only tourists like it." In Aravind Adiga's Man Booker–winning first novel, *The White Tiger,* the narrator declares. "Every man must make his own Benares," a way of saying that, for the up-wardly mobile and up-to-the-minute creature of New India, the Old City stands for all the ageless hierarchies and ancient rites that have to be pushed aside. Varanasi is the home of your grand-mother's grandmother's dusty superstitions, and the new global Indian purports to have no time for it.

At the river itself, on the rare day when the fog lifted, men were blowing conch shells to greet the dawn, and women were pounding clothes upon the stone steps to wash them. Saried fig-ures were stepping into the surging brown, and others were lifting their cupped hands to the rising sun. Varanasi, I thought, was a five-thousand-year-old man who may have put on an feuk shirt and acquired a Nokia but still takes the shirt off each morning to bathe in polluted waters and uses his new cell phone to download Vedic chants.

There is another sight that helps to underline this ancient dialec-tic. Indeed, Sarnath, more or less a suburb of Varanasi these days, is to some extent the product of the same back-and-forth. Born into the higher reaches of Hinduism, the young prince who be-came the Buddha walked away from all the abstraction and ritu-alism of Brahmin priests in order to find his own truth, just by stilling his mind and seeing what lies behind our pinwheeling thoughts and projections. After he came to his understanding in the town of Bodh Gaya, he traveled to Sarnath's Deer Park and outlined his eightfold path for seeing through suffering.

To travel from Varanasi to Sarnath today is to undertake a similar journey, and one that retraces a central shift in the history of philosophy. As soon as you move out into the country fields and narrow roads on the way to the little village, the roar and tumult of the holy city begin to vanish, and you see Buddhist temples from all the traditions—and buildings with names like the Society for Human Perception—peeping from behind the trees. A beautiful museum houses Buddhas excavated in the area over centuries. One minute you're in the midst of the whirligig shock of crackling flames and darkened lanes, and thirty minutes later you are in a large, quiet park where monks in yellow and gray and claret robes are seated silently on the grass, meditating before the Dhamekh Stupa, originally set up here by the emperor Ashoka 249 years before the birth of Christ.

Because the Dalai Lama was about to offer teachings nearby, the pleasant park around the 143-foot stupa had been transformed into a busy, merry Tibetan settlement. As I looked out on the park, some Vietnamese nuns in triangular bamboo hats joined the Tibetans to pay their silent respects, while a Mongolian— striking in topknot and beard and rich silk robes—roared out his prayers. I went to listen to the Dalai Lama talk about the bodhisattva way of life, and when he was finished, the little lanes of the settlement filled with so many red-robed monks that it felt as if we had all ended up in Lhasa when it was a center of the Buddhist world.

On my arrival in Varanasi, it had seemed impossible to pull myself out of its hypnotic spell, its constant movement, its air of danger around the flames, where so many men (and it seemed to be all men) were waiting in such a state of restless energy that I could feel the sense of violence just below the surface of the Indian communion, in which a spark of misunderstanding can quickly turn into a blaze. On my third day in the city, my bicycle rickshaw ran right into a procession for the Shia festival of Muharram, in which thousands of bare-chested Muslim boys were waving swords, shouting slogans of defiance, and carrying through the narrow, jam-packed streets ten-foot poles and silver-tinseled shrines that looked certain to collapse on us all at any moment. Two days later, the monthlong period of mourning was still blocking traffic.

But as the days went on, I realized that all I really had to do was sit and let life along the riverbank unfold around me. A crow was perched on a placid cow, now and then pecking bits of seed off the animal's cheek. A holy man fielded a cricket ball in the river and flung it back to the boys who had set up a high-speed game along the banks. Gypsies from the backpack trail drifted by, swathed in scarves and shawls.

I had been determined not to fall under the city's spell, nor to repeat the lines that so many millions of visitors have uttered, changelessly, for more centuries than I can count. I knew that Varanasi—India to the max—would stretch credulity in every direction, and I told myself to stay clear and alert, on the throne of pure reason. A part of me, lapsed Hindu, longed to stand apart. But as I kept returning to the ghats, I found myself thinking along lines I'd never explored before. Standing by the bonfires, suddenly noting how silent all the men around me were—the clamor was coming from elsewhere—I started to imagine what it would feel like to see a lover's body crumbling and crackling before my eyes, the shoulder I had grown used to holding every day for twenty years reduced to ash. I started to think about what one does with remains, and what exactly they mean (or don't). I felt the truth of the Buddhist exercises my friends sometimes spoke about, of seeing in every beautiful model the skeleton beneath the fancy covering.

I began to walk south along the river then, till I came to the other burning ghat—orange flames lighting up the surrounding buildings with their glow—and as I kept walking, the path grew deserted and dark till the only light came from far above, where a candle was flickering inside a rounded shrine. I walked on and on, deeper into the dark, knowing the steps and walkways of the city so well by now that I could dodge the areas where the water buffalo were wont to relieve themselves, and knew how not to get tangled in the kite strings of the little boys who raced along the riverbank in the uncertain light as if to tangle us all up in Varanasi itself. The decaying palaces up above, with their hollowed-out windows and interiors stuffed with refuse, or with huddled bodies, looked, when a light came on, like the homes of celebrants at some great festival who had long passed on—ghost houses.

That death could be a shrine before which everyone pays homage; that holy things, as a tour guide says in Shusaku Endo's haunting Varanasi novel, *Deep River*, do not have to be pretty things; that all of us are flowing on a river in which we will be picked up and brought into a larger current; and that there can be flames marking the fires of heaven as much as of hell—all played havoc with what I thought I knew.

A crossing ground, I began to think, is not just where the dead move on to something else but where the living are carried off to another plane, and where thought and sensation themselves are turned around. "For Hindus," I had read in the work of the great Varanasi scholar Diana L. Eck, "death is not the opposite of life; it is, rather, the opposite of birth"—akin, perhaps, to leaving a cinema by a different door than the one you came in by.

The following morning I ran into my guide from my first day, always so eager to show visitors the beauties of his city.

"How are you, my friend?" I called.

"So good, sir. It is a beautiful day. More warm. No fog. Visibility is good."

"So you think the curse is lifted?"

"Oh yes, sir. This all means it is the coming of spring."

The next morning, my last, I awoke to find the whole city covered in a pall of mist so thick that the ghostly towers and palaces I could see from my room seemed to have unmade themselves in the dark. Planes would not be able to take off or land. Trains would be delayed twenty hours or more. Vehicles would crash into one another, with fatal results. Down by the river, I could not see thirty feet in front of me, so that the smoke from all the fires— and winter fog and pollution—made every figure I saw look like a visitor from another world. It could seem as if we were all trapped now, spellbound in this sleeping world, and that the dense, feverish, self-contained model of the universe was inside our bones and had become our destiny, our home.

MARK JARMAN

The Teachable Moment

John 18:38

Pilate questioned Jesus.
Jesus questioned back.
Pilate questioned him again—
The cool Socratic tack.

Their repartee was candid,
A pointed give-and-take.
It was not clear if its last word
Was freely willed or fated.

When Jesus chose to answer
And give the reason why,
Pilate asked him, "What is truth?"

～

Enough about the distant posting among barbarians,
Enough about having to arbitrate their quarrels,
Enough about their religions—about any religion—
Enough about whatever was going on at home, with the family,

When it came time for the intellectual push and pull
He had everything covered, riposte and response,
The tools of dialectic, a question for a question.
He said no more to this princeling of an obscure cause
But turned to the crowd and asked them what they wanted.
Did he win the debate? Do as fated? Make a cosmic mistake?

ॐ

Inside me I believe there is
A Pilate questioning Jesus
And a Jesus answering.
Or no Pilate. Or no Jesus.

ॐ

These two people, powers of their time,
Faced off like a major city and an earthquake.
The city has endured so many earthquakes,
The earthquake's always virgin with a city.
One says it's coming. One must rather doubt it.
And the city shakes down on its tens of thousands.
But here's the thing: the city is rebuilt
With the same name, perhaps with earthquake codes.
The earthquake will not come again for centuries.
And the city stands again, where it has stood.
No wonder the city doubts its own destruction.
How can you live, except to doubt your death?

ॐ

To feel your whole body is the truth,
To feel you are the truth and more than truth,
Your feet, your toes, the shinbone and the knee
Are true and more than true, to be the truth,

Standing on your own feet, and riding hips
As true as they were ever meant to be,
The rest going upward, through the groin,
The functional, true genitals, the belly
Spread with its pubic hair all true, all true,
And up the ridged divided abdomen,
Between the nipples, truly loving touch,
The clavicles with their delicacy and music,
The arms and hands and fingers with their reach,
The tower of the neck, as Solomon says,
The identifiable face, *your* face,
The ears to bear both the outer and inner voices,
The mouth, the speaker of the truth, the nose,
True to its compass bearings, smelling falsehoods,
The eyes looking into the puzzled eyes
Of one you've scared into urgent reasoning—
To feel that you embody the whole truth
And then to know that truth is going to be beaten,
Beaten to the bone, skeletonized,
And hang like a limp rag, as dead as rope—
To be this truth completely, unadorned,
Real as the hand before another's face,
And have that other still say, "What is truth?"

            ॐ

But there is more.
There's always more.
The score's not settled.
There is more.

One shuts the door.
One strikes the door,

Worried, nettled,
Outside the door.

What is truth for?
What is it for
For those who worry
What it is for?

Who pace the floor,
The shifting floor
Of air and fury,
Like a classroom floor.

Who mark the hour,
The frozen hour
Of the last word,
As the first hour?

And what is power
That once was power
In an old word
With a new power?

         ℐ

The teachable moment.
The last judgment occurring
Again and again as a teachable moment.
But what moment ever lasted long enough
To learn anything? This moment.

CHARLES JOHNSON

Welcome to Wedgwood

FROM *Shambhala Sun*

> *A new Rasmussen Reports survey finds that 69 percent of Americans think their fellow countrymen are becoming ruder and less civilized. Men are much more likely than women to have confronted someone over their rude behavior, though more women than men think sales and service personnel are ruder than they were a decade ago. Adults over age fifty are more likely than their younger counterparts to think it is rude for someone sitting next to them in public to talk on their cell phone.*

> I have learned silence from the talkative, toleration
> from the intolerant, and kindness from the unkind;
> yet, strange I am ungrateful to those teachers.
> —KAHLIL GIBRAN

THE TROUBLE STARTED ON A LATE AFTERNOON IN SEPTEMBER. IT was around 6 p.m., and I was sitting under one of the trees in my backyard, watching a brace of pigeons splash wildly around in our stone bird bath, beneath which a stone head of the Buddha rose up from the grass. My dog Nova, a West Highland white terrier, rested peacefully nearby. I've always loved this hour of the day, when the spill of late afternoon light, so ethereal, filtered through old-growth trees in Wedgwood, a neighborhood of gentle hills and slopes at the edge of strip malls, burger joints, auto dealers, and Rick's topless nightclub in Lake City. But here you never felt you were in a big city—with all those big city problems—because before the Second World War this area used to be an orchard filled with more apple, pear, and plum trees than people, and all that lush plumage absorbed the whoosh of traffic on Lake City Way. Here, traffic moved along at thirty miles an hour. Years ago, it was outside the city limits, and so mailboxes were not attached to our houses but instead were out on the street, which had no sidewalks. It's been called a "Prunes and Raisins" neighborhood, but don't ask me why. All I know is that the spirit of place in Wedgwood (named after the English china), where I've lived for half my life, was that of a quiet, hidden oasis within Seattle, inhabited mainly by older, retired people like myself who all owned dogs, and quite a few college professors since it was only two miles from the University of Washington. A wonderful place, if you enjoyed walking. But here and there things had begun to change. Younger people were moving in, and some years ago the police raided a home that someone had turned into a meth lab. Yet and still, violence in Wedgwood was rare.

So that afternoon, I sat in a lazy lotus posture under an evergreen tree, the forefingers on each hand tipped against my thumbs, thinking about images from a new poem, "The Ear Is an Organ Made for Love," I'd received via email from my friend Ethelbert Miller. Behind me, floating on an almost hymnal silence, a few soothing notes sounded from the wood chimes hanging from my house, accompanied by bird flutter and the rustle of leaves at about ten decibels. Up above, the light seemed captured in cloud puffs, which looked luminous, as if they held candles within. The soughing of the wind in the trees was like rushing water. I began to slowly drift into meditation, hoping today would bring at least a tidbit of spiritual discovery, but no sooner than I'd closed my eyes and felt the outside world fall away, the air was shattered by a hair-raising explosion of music booming from stereo speakers somewhere nearby, like a clap of thunder or a volcano exploding. Now, I love music, especially soft jazz, but only at certain, special hours of the day. This was heavy metal techno-pounding at 120 decibels, alternating with acid rock, and sprinkled with gangster rap that sounded to my ear like rhymed shouting. And it *did* rock—and shock—the neighborhood with a tsunami of inquietude. Its energy was five billion times greater than that from the wood chimes. It compressed the air around me and clogged my consciousness. I looked at Nova, and behind his quiet, blackberry eyes he seemed to be thinking, "What is *that*, boss?"

"Our new neighbors," I said. "We haven't introduced ourselves to them yet, but I guess they're having a party."

You have to understand, I talk to my dog all the time, which is better than talking to myself and being embarrassed if someone caught me doing that, and he never says a word back, which is no doubt one of the reasons why people love dogs.

One or two hours went by, and we listened helplessly as the exhausting, emotionally draining sound yeasted to 130 decibels, moving in concentric spheres from my neighbor's place, covering blocks in every direction like smog or pollution or an oil spill, and just as toxic and rude, as enveloping and inescapable as the Old Testament voice of God when He was having a bad day. And now, suddenly, *I* was having a bad day. This was exactly the opposite of the tranquillity I wanted, but there was no escaping the bass beat that reverberated in my bones, the energy of the shrill profanity and angry lyrics as they assaulted the penetralia of my eardrums, traveling down to the tiny, delicate hairs of the cochlea, and from there to the sensitive, sympathetic nervous system that directed the tremors straight into my brain. Unlike an unpleasant vision, from which I could turn away or close my eyes, wave upon wave of oscillations passed right through my hands when I held them against the sides of my head. The music, if I may call it that, was intrusive, infectious, wild, sensual, pagan, orgasmic, jangling, indecent, and filled me with foreign emotions not of my own making, completely overwhelming and washing away my thoughts and the silent, inner speech we all experience when our soul talks to itself.

I no longer recognized Wedgwood as my neighborhood. All its virtues—the magnificent views of Lake Washington and the Cascade Mountain Range, its old world charm—had vanished, and I felt as if I'd been suddenly teleported to Belltown at 11 on a Saturday night. I wondered if the Generation X new arrivals knew how fragile our ears are, and how many scientific studies indicated that noise pollution interfered with learning, lowered math and reading scores, and was responsible for high blood pressure, dry mouth, blindness, muscular contractions, neurosis, heart disease, peptic ulcers, constipation, premature ejaculation, reduced libido, insomnia, congenital birth defects, and even death.

Now darkness had fallen, but still the pulsions continued across the street, surrounding my house like a hand squeezing a wineglass on the verge of shattering. My ears felt like they wanted to bleed. And only heaven knows how Nova was feeling, since his hearing was four times more sensitive than mine. I shook my head at the thought of what a dangerously noisy species we humans are with our clanking, humming, churning machinery and motorcars, our loud music and household appliances with their anapestic beat, and fire sirens wailing. Walking into the house, I saw my wife coming down the stairs, wearing her round reading glasses and looking dazed. At sixty-two, she was slightly hard of hearing in one ear, but the stramash had shaken her and made her feel exiled from the familiar, too. She started shutting all our windows. But that didn't help. The sound curdled the air inside our house, and her sore ears were burning as badly as mine. From the porch we could see cars lining the street, beer cans thrown into the bushes, and from our neighbor's property there wafted pungent clouds of Purple Haze and Hawaii Skunk marijuana.

"I was reading the Book of Psalms in bed," my wife said, "but I couldn't concentrate with all that noise. What do you think we should do?"

"Call 911?"

 "Oh, no!" she said. Unlike Nova, she *did* talk back to me. "They're just kids. We were kids once, remember?" Then suddenly her lips pouted and she looked hurt. "Why are you shouting at me?"

"Was I shouting?"

"Yes," she said. "You were yelling at me."

I didn't realize how much I'd raised my voice in order to be heard over the mind-blinding music blaring outside—she was, after all, only two feet away from me. Or that the noise, despite all my decades of spiritual practice, could so quickly make me feel spent and flammable and reveal an irascible side of me to my wife neither of us had seen in forty years of marriage. I was no longer myself, though I suspected this was a teachable moment, as politicians say, and there was a lesson to be learned here but, so help me, I just wasn't getting it. I apologized to my wife. I knew she was right, as usual. We shouldn't call the police. This was a difficult situation that had to be handled with delicacy, but I was confident that I could be as magnanimous and civilized as any post-Enlightenment, Western man who had control over himself after thirty years of meditation on his mushroom-shaped cushion. But that didn't mean I couldn't try to escape for awhile. I decided this was a good time to go shopping. I stepped outside, where the rough, pounding sound almost knocked me to my knees. The traumatizing waves were so thick I felt I was moving through a haze of heat, or underwater. I wondered, who *are* these rude people? These invaders? I strapped Nova into my Jeep Wrangler and, with my wife's list of groceries in the hip pocket of my jeans—milk, canned vegetables, paper towels, a chocolate cake to celebrate the birthday of one of her friends at Mount Zion Baptist Church, and dog treats—we fled into the night, or more precisely, to the QFC on 35th Avenue.

As the Doppler effect kicked in, as I put half a mile between myself and ground zero, as the pitch declined, I felt less agitated, though there was a slight ringing and seashell sound in my ears, lingering like a low-grade fever. For all the discomfort I was feeling, I also felt something else: namely, how sound and silence, so universal in our lives as to normally be ignored, were profound mysteries I'd never properly understood or respected until now, when the absence of one and the presence of the other was so badly disrupting my life.

Compared to my street, the supermarket, surrounded by eateries and ale houses, was mercifully quiet. I went down the aisles, collecting items we needed, remembering that just one month ago a QFC employee charged with domestic violence for choking his mother unconscious was killed in this supermarket when he fought the police who came to arrest him. I kept thinking, as I picked items off the shelves, *Are those vibes still in this store?* (You can probably tell I came of age in the sixties.) I dismissed that thought, and then stood patiently in the checkout line behind five other customers, one being a plump, elderly woman with frosted hair who, of course, had to pay by writing a check, which seemed to take forever. I swear, I think she was balancing her checking account or calculating her quarterly taxes, there at the front of the line. I could imagine her drinking a hot cup of Ovaltine before going to bed and having ninety-seven cats in her midcentury Wedgwood home. I kept wondering why someone didn't call for another cashier—or even better, two—to handle this line of people backed up into the aisles. Finally, after ten minutes it was my turn. The cashier was a genial young man whose eyes behind his wire-framed glasses looked glazed from ringing up so many customers, but he was trying to be cheerful. He took my QFC Advantage card, and said, "So how is *your* day going?"

Usually, I enjoy chatting with people behind the cash register, finding out a little about their lives, letting them know they're people in my community I care about and not just faceless objects to me. I try to be patient, reciting my mantra if I have a long wait in a public place. But right then I said, in spite of myself, "What the hell do you care?"

That reply shocked him as much as it did me. I tried to recover. I said, "Sorry! I didn't *mean* that. I think I'm vibrating too fast."

He cut his eyes my way. "Excuse me?"

"Long story. Never mind."

"You want paper or plastic?"

My voice slipped a scale. "Paper . . . please."

That would prove to be a mistake.

I hurried out of QFC, pushing my little gray cart with four bags of groceries as quickly as I could, and stopped at Rite-Aid across the street to buy earplugs for my wife and myself. It was now 9:30 p.m. Driving home, I was praying the neighbor's party was over, but to my surprise, yet somehow not to my surprise, I felt—even though my ears were plugged—the density in the air before I heard the humping arcs still flooding the neighborhood like a broken water main. Even worse, when I downshifted into my driveway, I had to hit the brakes because another car was parked in *my space*. My neighbor's guests had filled the street with their vehicles. The one in my driveway, a Chevrolet Blazer, had a skull-and-bones decal in the back window, and under that a bumper sticker that said, "You Can Kiss The Crack Below My Back." My first impulse was to let the air out of its tires, but then realized that would only keep it in my driveway longer.

So I parked two blocks away. I looped Nova's nylon leash around my left wrist, loaded up my arms as high as my chin with four heavy bags of food, and started tramping slowly uphill back to my house. That's when fat raindrops began to fall. By the time I was thirty feet from my front door, the paper bags were soaking wet and falling apart. Ten feet from the door, Nova realized we were almost home. He sprang for the steps—Westies hate to get wet—and that snapped my left arm straight out, which sent cans of sliced pineapples, soup, and tomatoes, bottles of maple syrup and milk, and bags of raisins, potatoes, and rice cascading back down the declivity, littering the street like confetti or a landfill. For the longest time, I stood there, head tipped and sopping wet, watching my neighbor's guests flee inside to escape the rain, lost in the whorl of violent, invisible vibrations, and I was disabused forever of the vanity that three decades of practicing meditation had made me too civilized, too cultivated, too mellow to be vulnerable to or victimized by fugitive thoughts—anger, desire, self-pity, pettiness—triggered in me from things outside. These would always arise, I saw, even without noise pollution.

Then, all at once, the loud music stopped.

Dragging my dog behind me, I slogged across the street, so tired I couldn't see straight. I climbed my new neighbor's stairs, and banged my fist on the front door. After a moment it opened, and standing there with a can of Budweiser in his right hand was possibly the most physically fit young man I'd ever seen. I placed his age at thirty. Maybe thirty-five. In other words, he was young enough to be my son. His short hair was a military buzz cut, his *ears*

T-shirt olive-colored, his ears large enough for him to wiggle if he wanted to, like President Obama's, and on his arm I saw a tattoo for the Fourth Brigade of the Second Infantry Division he'd served with at Fort Lewis-McChord. He looked me up and down as I stood dripping on his doorstep, and politely said:

"Yes, sir? Can I help you?"

"We need to talk," I said.

He squinted his eyes as if trying to read my lips. Then he put one hand behind his ear like an old, old man who'd lost his hearing aid, or someone who'd been a blacksmith all his life. "What did you say, sir?"

I was less than a foot away from him. I felt like I was coming to from a dream. A profound sadness swept over me, dousing my anger, for I understood the unnecessary tragedy of tinnitus in someone so young. His was maybe the result of a recent tour in Iraq or Afghanistan, perhaps from an IED. I felt humbled. I did not judge him or myself now, because he had taught me how to listen better. I gestured with one finger held up for him to wait a moment, and went back into the downpour. On the street, I found what I was looking for, grateful that its plastic lid had kept it from being ruined by the rain. I climbed the steps again.

"Thank you," I said, giving him the chocolate cake. "And welcome to Wedgwood."

JAMES LASDUN

Unbuilt Jerusalem

FROM *Harper's Magazine*

WHEN THE ISRAELI GOVERNMENT ANNOUNCED PLANS LAST
March to build 1,600 new homes in East Jerusalem, it prompted
a furious reaction from both the Palestinians and the United
States. I wasn't following the story closely, but a subplot that sur-
faced a few days after the announcement plunged me unexpect-
edly into an episode of family history that I hadn't thought about
for years.

At issue was a synagogue, the Hurva, that had been the Jew-
ish Quarter's main religious building until it was destroyed in
1948. After lying in ruins for sixty years, it had been rebuilt and
was about to be officially reopened. Although the *New York Times*
called it "a case of unfortunate timing," many Palestinians saw an
explicit link between the settlements in East Jerusalem and the
new synagogue. Hamas called for a "day of rage." Fatah accused
the Israelis of "playing with fire." Arab Knesset members warned
of a third Intifada. Three thousand security personnel were put
on alert for the opening ceremony.

Why the rebuilding of a synagogue in the Jewish Quarter
should have become part of the settlement dispute was a little
puzzling, but it was the architectural rather than the political
aspect of the story that interested me at first.

In 1973, my father, Denys Lasdun, an architect who had designed several prominent buildings in England including the Royal National Theatre, was commissioned to design a new synagogue on the site of the Hurva ruins. For several years he shuttled back and forth between London and Jerusalem, working on the plans.

He wasn't the first architect involved. Louis Kahn had done designs for the building before he died in 1974. Kahn and my father had both served on Jerusalem mayor Teddy Kollek's international advisory board, the Jerusalem Committee, set up after the Six-Day War. The choice of these modernists indicates the nature of Kollek's aesthetic ambitions for the building and the city. This was to be a statement: a showpiece for a reunited, progressive, globally minded Jerusalem.

But nothing came of either Kahn's or my father's plans. What had been built instead after all these years was something so far from Kollek's vision as to amount to a direct repudiation of it. It was a copy, an exact replica of the Ottoman original.

The synagogue was destroyed not once but twice, and has spent more of its life as rubble than upright. It was first built in 1700, by Polish emigrants. Money for the construction was borrowed from the Arab community, but after a few years the congregation defaulted on its debt and creditors tore down the building, at which point it acquired its present, fateful name; *hurva* is Hebrew for "ruin."

Another synagogue was built on the site, completed in 1864 by followers of a Lithuanian rabbi known as the Vilna Gaon, a revered figure in orthodox Judaism. This building, a domed structure designed by the Turkish sultan's own architect, dominated the skyline of the Jewish Quarter and came to be regarded as the official religious center of Jewish Jerusalem. Theodor Herzl and

Ze'ev Jabotinsky spoke there. The first British high commissioner of Palestine, Sir Herbert Samuel, paid a ceremonial visit in 1920. And in 1948, during the Arab-Israeli war, it was shelled by the Jordanian army.

Here the story becomes stranger. There is a prophecy attributed to the Vilna Gaon that states that three versions of the Hurva would be built, and that the completion of the third would bring about the rebuilding of the Temple in Jerusalem. Rebuilding the Temple (itself twice destroyed, first by the Babylonians, then by the Romans) is a motif in the climactic scenarios of all kinds of cults and sects, Christian as well as Jewish. We are in the realm of baroque eschatology here, but there is probably no spot on earth where religious fantasy has more combustible potential than the small area of Jerusalem encompassing the Temple Mount and the Jewish Quarter. The Vilna Gaon's prophecy was cited by Hamas and Fatah as a principal reason for denouncing the Hurva in its present, third, incarnation. In the light of this prophecy, they claimed, the rebuilding of the synagogue constituted a threat to the two landmarks currently occupying the Temple Mount (or al-Haram ash-Sharif, as Muslims call it): the Al Aqsa Mosque and the Dome of the Rock.

As far as I know, neither Kollek nor Kahn nor my father knew about the Vilna Gaon's prophecy. They were all fairly worldly types, and the political discourse was relatively secular in those days, even in Jerusalem. But whether they knew it or not, they were all engaged for a time in an endeavor that seems, in retrospect, to have had a distinct tinge of the apocalypse about it.

I visited the Victoria and Albert Museum's architectural collection last September, to look at the Hurva papers in my father's archive. The archivist had set out the files in the Architecture Study Room, an airy space with glare screens on tall windows and scholars working at long tables in a civilized hush that made me nostalgic for London (I left twenty years ago). The memories brought back by the archive itself were equally fond, but more turbulent. My father's insistence on complete artistic control over all aspects of the jobs he took on, combined with the fact that most of these jobs were large-scale public buildings, with politicians and other interfering types on the steering committees, made for a generally embattled atmosphere around him. I had left home by the time he got Kollek's commission, but the archive proved that the Hurva job was no exception. Old fights reconstituted themselves from the papers in the thick file boxes; old storms boiled back up among telexes about fee schedules and meetings with city engineers.

The main conflict concerned Kollek's insistence, for PR purposes, on presenting the scheme as a joint effort with an Israeli architect. Liaising with a local architect is normal on any overseas job, and my father was fine with that, but he drew the line at actual collaboration. THERE CAN BE NO QUESTION OF DESIGN BY COMMITTEE, he thunders by telex to Jerusalem. A formula is agreed on, but then the *Jerusalem Post* demotes the Israeli architect in an article on the project. Kollek blames my father, and a memo records a chill in relations: "TK was barely civil presumably because he was cross about press reference." A day later my father phones Kollek to discuss the matter: "TK exploded that he was not interested in phone calls about this sort of thing and that he found DL a most difficult man to deal with." "DL," my indignant father has his secretary type, "is not prepared to tolerate any further outbursts from TK of this nature and the job must now be regarded as problematical." Ronald Dworkin, the American jurist and a friend of my father's, is brought in as an informal intermediary: "Dworkin and wife just back from Jerusalem. They had looked at Hurva site and talked to TK. . . . While TK admits

S [the Israeli architect] may not be the greatest architect in the world, he must present the authorship as one of 'collaboration.' " Bobbing on this choppy sea is the unfortunate "S," a Mr. Schen- or Schon- or Schoenberger (nobody can get his name right), who falls sick a year into the conflict and resolves it, inadvertently, by dying.

My father was Jewish, but he had grown up in an assimilated household, converted to Christianity, lapsed, and even though he always publicly identified as a Jew, his real religion was archi- tecture, with Hawksmoor and Wren for his Old Testament and Le Corbusier for the New. At any rate he knew little about Juda- ism and next to nothing about synagogues. To learn about the traditions he talked to rabbis and historians and brought in a young scholar, Robert van Pelt, for weekly lunchtime meetings. While van Pelt talked about temples, altars, bimahs, and arks, my father would furiously scribble notes and diagrams on the paper tablecloth. At the end of each meal the tablecloth—wine stains, crumbs, and all—was handed to the office secretary, and the fol- lowing week a sheaf of neatly typed notes would be presented to van Pelt, who was required to read them and (my father being somewhat tyrannical about record-keeping) sign them.

The tablecloths aren't in the archive, but the notes are, and along with the other advisory memos they chart the evolution of the design, which went through two main phases. The first, re- ferred to as the "stratified scheme," was a close echo of my father's prior work, especially the National Theatre, in which long strata are used to tie the building visually to the city around it, the new reaching out into the old. The resemblance was strong enough for him to have worried that he would be accused of repeating himself, and he evidently asked his advisers to supply historical precedents. "Hurva looks like Theatre," one of them writes, "just as Palladio's churches share features with his villas." Enthusiastic lines in my father's soft-leaded pencil stripe the margin next to this unabashedly grandiose note, but in the end the design didn't satisfy him and he scrapped it, a year's work tossed, embarking instead on the "vertical scheme" that formed his final plan. Four pairs of thin, square, stone-faced towers stand sentinel over the four sides of a slab-roofed central space containing the ark and bimah. Van Pelt noted an affinity between its basic form and that of ancient Jewish altars. He brought my father pictures of these curious rectangular structures with their four "horns," and these seem to have encouraged the new approach.

My father wasn't easily satisfied by his own work, but I remember that he was pleased with the Hurva design. Kollek seemed happy too. Three years into the job, he writes warmly, "You know that the Hurva is one of my dreams."

Sitting in the archive, I couldn't help but hear the valedictory note in that, as if Kollek already half knew it wasn't going to be built. But he had approved its construction; he had even conducted a cornerstone-laying ceremony with the president of Israel, and by 1982 was only waiting for the go-ahead from the housing minister, who in turn was waiting for approval from the prime minister.

This never came. The trips, the telexes, the quarrels and reconciliations, the whole four-year agon of debate, reflection, and revision turned out to have been a waste of time. The prime minister at the time was Menachem Begin, and Begin had his own ideas for the synagogue. A clipping in the archive files from the *Jerusalem Post* makes it clear that the project is going to be shelved. What Begin wanted was a replica, and he had no intention of letting his housing minister sign off on anything else. Nineteen years after his death, the will of this deeply conservative figure appears to have prevailed.

· · ·

The pomegranates are ripening in Jerusalem. They hang over dusty gardens in the modern neighborhoods, and everywhere you go in the Old City there are juice stalls piled high with them. When the vendors cut them in half and crush them in their antique juicers, a thin, astringent liquid trickles out. It is very refreshing in the intense September heat of the crowded alleys but it also, I am told, lowers your blood pressure, which possibly accounts for the faint dizziness I have been feeling since I arrived.

This may also be an effect of being continually thrust up against questions that, as the Anglo-American offspring of two semi-Christianized Jews, I don't find easy to answer. What are you? Why are you here? To the Israelis I meet, I seem to be a source of particularly uneasy curiosity. Do I follow the British media (too hard on Israel) or the American (too soft)? My interest in the Hurva arouses vague dismay: is this going to be another embarrassment, like the disastrously named Museum of Tolerance, the proposed site of which turned out to be a Muslim cemetery?

Before I visit the Hurva itself, I climb up to the high roof of the Austrian Hospice, just inside the Damascus Gate, to view the dome on the skyline. It rises, shallow and unadorned, on the horizon; a distinctly Judaic presence among the crosses and crescent moons, though not, it seems to me, a particularly assertive one. It's much smaller than the three other cupolas: the Holy Sepulchre, the Al Aqsa, and the Dome of the Rock. Later I look at it from the Temple Mount. From there its dome does look a little more imposing, a sort of pale eye periscoping up above the Jewish Quarter. But on purely physical grounds it seems a stretch to regard it as any kind of threat to the mosques.

Louis Kahn's scheme, a vast, dark, slope-walled Egyptian temple held up by mighty stone pylons, with a processional walkway leading all the way across the Quarter to the Western Wall, would have loomed menacingly over the city. Kollek himself, though he admired the design's grandeur, was taken aback by its scale. "Should we in the Jewish Quarter," he muses in a letter, "have a building of major importance which 'competes' with the Mosque and Holy Sepulchre . . . ?" Kollek's diffident tone reflects the hesitancy that many Israelis felt at that time, between the two paths laid before them by the 1967 victories: triumphalism and restraint.

My father's plan would have kept to the footprint of the original structure. As I imagine its slim towers out there among the rooftops and minarets, I can't help thinking that his version of the building, his last major commission, would have looked pretty good.

But it was perhaps just as well for him that it wasn't built. One day, a few years into the project, he took me aside to show me a letter he'd been sent. It consisted of a photocopy of an article about his design, with the text blacked out, and handwritten words scrawled over the pictures. DANGER JEWS ABOUT was the first phrase I read. There were drawings of swastikas equaling Stars of David, sexual insults, and outright threats: IF YOU DESIGN THIS YOU WILL DIE PREMATURE DEATH. And there was that peculiarly nasty conflation of the roles of victim and oppressor that seems to distinguish anti-Semitic taunts from other kinds: HITLER WAS RIGHT TO GAS JEWS, on the one hand, and THIS IS JEW ECONOMY DIRTY PEOPLE ONLY KNOW HOW TO MASSACRE PEOPLE, on the other. AL QUDS. NOT THIS was written at the top along with the name JAWEED KARIM, presumably the sender.

I came across this letter in the archive and found it as disturbing as I had thirty years ago. My father had been shocked by it, naturally, and worried about how my mother would react (he decided we shouldn't tell her), but he didn't dwell on it, and it didn't cross his mind (or mine) to give any serious thought to what might have been the underlying grievance. Certainly, there was no discussion in his office about the political implications of the job: it simply didn't strike anyone as contentious.

Reinventing Jerusalem, a recent book by the British scholar and conservation architect Simone Ricca, makes the provocative case that the post-'67 reconstruction of the Jewish Quarter wasn't a restoration project so much as a calculated propaganda exercise that used demolition, expropriation, selective archaeology, and architectural trompe l'oeil to create the illusion of a much more substantial historic Jewish presence in the Old City than there had ever been, thereby justifying the Israeli takeover of East Jerusalem. As such, Ricca says, the reconstruction became a major source of inspiration for the settler movement that evolved soon after. Kollek, in Ricca's analysis, turns from enlightened visionary into a more dubious figure, hoodwinking the world into accepting that what he was doing was authentic restoration rather than the blatant manufacture of spurious heritage. The Western Wall's transformation into what Ricca calls "the central altar of the Israeli state" was a direct result of this exercise (before '67, the Wall had nothing like its present ceremonial significance). As for the Hurva, the idea that a single center ever existed for the city's fractious Jewish community was an invention of the secular "Ashkenazi elite" (the book's villains) who saw the project as a further opportunity to harness religious energies to a nationalist cause.

It is a complex, nuanced book; very thorough and, in the way of much academic writing about post-'67 Israel, rather merciless. It refrains, icily, from any attempt to enter the Israeli state of mind at that moment of seemingly miraculous victory over enemies who, if their rhetoric was to be believed, would very much have liked to destroy Israel altogether. How far it succeeds in undermining the legitimacy of Jewish Quarter reconstruction in general and the Hurva project in particular, I am not sure. Ricca makes much of the Jordanian army's claim that they blew up the synagogue in 1948 only after warning the Jewish command, via the Red Cross, that they would have no other option unless Jewish forces withdrew from the building, which they were using as a stronghold. This is well documented. What he doesn't mention is the equally well-documented fact that by 1967 the Jordanians had demolished or defaced all but one of the quarter's fifty-three other synagogues. And he omits the words of the Jordanian commander after the final retreat of Jewish forces following the destruction of the Hurva:

> For the first time in a thousand years not a single Jew remains in the Jewish Quarter. Not a single building remains intact. This makes the Jews' return here impossible.

Visitors are not warmly encouraged at the new Hurva. They may enter during prayers, or at appointed times in tour groups restricted to the women's gallery and the walkway around the dome. A gated lodge guards one main entrance, and a locked stairway bars the other. Between prayers the place functions as a school for its Misnagdim (non-Hasidic ultraorthodox) congregation, which would have surprised my father. "The orthodox Jews will mostly use their own synagogues," he wrote in a memo. "Hurva will be mostly for state occasions and tourists." From time to time, men in black velvet yarmulkes, white shirts, and sharp black suits are admitted through a side door, which closes firmly behind them. Security is of course a serious matter in this city, though I notice you can wander freely into the restored Sephardic synagogues down the road.

But the architect, Nahum Meltzer, is going to give me a private tour. Having strolled by the building a couple of times, I am expecting someone as crisp and starched as the congregants, so it is a surprise to find a disheveled, gray-haired man in a worn plaid shirt waiting for me. In addition to working on restoration projects, Meltzer has designed modern buildings, including an addition to the Knesset. By an odd coincidence, he once worked for my father in London. I warm to him quickly, all the more so because he seems to know in advance everything I am going to think about the synagogue, and not to mind too much. "It doesn't aspire to be architecture," he says with a melancholy smile before we set off. "Think of it as a bastard child of the Byzantine and the Ottoman." It amuses him that the original of this Jewish landmark was designed by a Muslim.

He offers to show me some of his favorite spots in the Old City before we go into the synagogue, and we take a meandering route past crumbling Mamluk palaces, into the serene Crusader church of St. Anne's, and back along the Via Dolorosa, squeezing past groups of pilgrims bowed under heavy crosses. The Christians here seem to inhabit a different universe from the Jews and Muslims; spatially contingent but projected from another time, their dramas and massacres occurring elsewhere, in the deep past or future. A different kind of temporal confusion occurs as you enter the Jewish Quarter. The buildings are modern, but faced in the ancient-looking sand-gold Jerusalem stone that is statutory for all new construction. It is easy on the eye but creates a slightly unreal, stage-set atmosphere. The human element adds to the effect. Kollek's "Ashkenazi elite" apparently had a secular population in mind when they rebuilt the area, but that group was quickly superseded by various Haredim sects, whose eclectic period gear—Prince Albert frock coats, silken knee breeches, side locks, and shaven heads under kippas topped by rakish black hats or massive beaver crowns; the whole (erroneously named) "Polish

Count" look, complicated by tassels and tallits and leather-strapped phylacteries, and worn on a motor scooter or while chatting on a cell phone—effects a total collapsing of eras.

Most of the Old City is too densely settled for its buildings to be experienced in the round. Even the monumental Church of the Holy Sepulchre is something you piece together from angled glimpses. The Hurva, in its previous incarnation, was similarly crowded-in, but the replica stands with its back to an empty piazza, looking both averted and exposed. It, too, is faced in Jerusalem stone, but of a whiter shade than its neighbors, which makes it look eerily new, while its form—the plain dome supported on a squat cube of four wide arches, with a chunky tower at each corner—is clearly old, so that the eye doesn't at first know what to make of it.

We enter through golden doors. Students blink up from their texts; mildly affronted, it seems, by our presence, until they realize one of the intruders is their esteemed architect. Respect is shown, but Meltzer tells me quietly that relations have been strained ever since he talked to the press about the congregation's less than welcoming attitude toward the public.

We look around the tall white interior with its painted panels and stained-glass windows. Meltzer points out where stones from the original ruin have been incorporated into the new concrete walls. He tells me about the artisans who carved and gilded the elaborate bimah and made the cast-iron balustrades. The craftsmanship looks very fine, but I am uncomfortably aware of how much my father would have loathed it all.

"Replica sterile unworthy," goes a handwritten note in his archive. "Context/piazza changed therefore phoney. . . . Remembering the past is not the same as being in the past." The use of modern techniques and materials to rebuild a nineteenth-century structure whose modest charm derived largely from its visibly ramshackle construction would have struck him as a singularly meaningless exercise. Arches and domes made from cast, precision-set concrete have a machine-age smoothness that no amount of hand-distressed stone cladding can disguise. (The original dome was honeycombed by clay bottles for reinforcement, and you can make out its bobbled unevenness in old photographs.) The fact that an elevator has been installed inside, and that a tower section from the original has been omitted to give a view to the Temple Mount, adds a note of capricious inconsistency that further weakens any case for "authenticity."

All this is clearly beside the point. Accurate or not, a replica is what has been built, and the consensus is that it was the only option that ever stood a chance. David Kroyanker, who has written extensively on Jerusalem architecture, told me he didn't like Kahn's scheme, adding bluntly, "I didn't like your father's either." Both, in his view, were too provocative—for aesthetically conservative Jews as well as for politically wary Palestinians—to have made it past the planning stage. He praised the meticulous detail of Meltzer's reconstruction and has given it his blessing. Esther Zandberg, *Haaretz*'s architecture critic, considers the replica cowardly but, again, the only buildable solution. Though no admirer of Begin, she credits him with understanding that an architectural non-statement would be the only way to neutralize opposition.

History, so far, has proved Begin right. Despite the dire words of Hamas and Fatah, the synagogue's reopening last March went smoothly. There were small protests away from the site, but the "day of rage" turned out to be a day of indifference. None of the Palestinians I spoke with had any interest in discussing the building. It simply wasn't a battle they wanted to fight. Call it a sleight of hand, an intervention in the past, but the synagogue has rematerialized as if it had never been destroyed. The mediocrity of the original design acts as a further cloak of invisibility over its pale double. Nobody sees it. Nobody cares. End of story.

But there remains something mysterious about the project. Kollek's lofty civic ambitions were long ago abandoned, so what has kept it alive all these years? Restoration for its own sake hardly seems sufficient as a motivating force. Could there be any merit in the view of the Hurva as part of some larger, ongoing preoccupation with the Temple Mount? I asked Kroyanker whether, given the curious connection between the two institutions, rebuilding the synagogue might amount to a proxy action for rebuilding the Temple: a kind of architectural gesture of yearning. He answered gloomily that for some people it undoubtedly was. He showed me the catalogue from an exhibition he had curated, called Unbuilt Jerusalem. Along with my father's and Louis Kahn's Hurva schemes, the exhibition featured ornately detailed Third Temple models built by local enthusiasts. There is a thriving Third Temple subculture in Jerusalem. Souvenir shops in the Jewish Quarter sell Third Temple table mats, holographic artist's impressions, even priestly garments. Last April, the director of the Temple Institute tried to sacrifice a goat outside the Hurva, having been turned away from the Temple Mount itself. It is all fairly crazy. High above the Western Wall Plaza, a vast, glass-encased golden menorah stands ready to be installed in the Temple when its hour comes round. "May it be rebuilt speedily and in our days," goes the legend beneath it. It was paid for by the main donor for the reconstruction of the Hurva.

Perhaps it's just a literary prejudice of mine to find the notion of any kind of double—architectural as much as human—inherently baleful. But there is no escaping a certain oppressive aura about this new-old building. The locked gates have aroused resentment among the remaining nonorthodox inhabitants of the quarter. The Hurva's rabbi, Simcha HaCohen Kook, comes from the same prominent rabbinical family as Zvi Yehuda Kook, founder of Gush Emunim, the religious settler movement. His appointment was controversial, even within the Jewish Quarter. I tried to interview Rabbi Kook at the synagogue. A very polite young man with a pistol took my number at the gate, but nobody called.

"I fully believe that we will witness the creation of a religious and spiritual focus for world Jewry," Kollek wrote to my father in 1979. He appointed a religious adviser to consult on Jewish law concerning sacred ruins, and among the precepts the adviser passed on was one stating that when a destroyed synagogue is to be rebuilt, "its beauty and glory should be increased." Perhaps there was a moment when such innocently expansive hopes could be seriously entertained in Jerusalem, but that moment has clearly passed.

At Ben Gurion airport I run into Nahum Meltzer again, on his way to visit a son in London. He tells me that plans are afoot for the rebuilding of another historic synagogue destroyed by the Jordanians, the Hasidic Tiferet Yisrael. It, too, will be a replica.

SY MONTGOMERY

Deep Intellect

FROM *Orion*

ON AN UNSEASONABLY WARM DAY IN THE MIDDLE OF MARCH, I traveled from New Hampshire to the moist, dim sanctuary of the New England Aquarium, hoping to touch an alternate reality. I came to meet Athena, the aquarium's forty-pound, five-foot-long, two-and-a-half-year-old giant Pacific octopus.

For me, it was a momentous occasion. I have always loved octopuses. No sci-fi alien is so startlingly strange. Here is someone who, even if she grows to one hundred pounds and stretches more than eight feet long, could still squeeze her boneless body through an opening the size of an orange; an animal whose eight arms are covered with thousands of suckers that taste as well as feel; a mollusk with a beak like a parrot and venom like a snake and a tongue covered with teeth; a creature who can shape-shift, change color, and squirt ink. But most intriguing of all, recent research indicates that octopuses are remarkably intelligent.

Many times I have stood mesmerized by an aquarium tank, wondering, as I stared into the horizontal pupils of an octopus's large, prominent eyes, if she was staring back at me—and if so, what was she thinking?

Not long ago, a question like this would have seemed foolish, if not crazy. How can an octopus know anything, much less form an opinion? Octopuses are, after all, "only" invertebrates—they don't even belong with the insects, some of whom, like dragonflies and dung beetles, at least seem to show some smarts. Octopuses are classified within the invertebrates in the mollusk family; and many mollusks, like clams, have no brain.

Only recently have scientists accorded chimpanzees, so closely related to humans we can share blood transfusions, the dignity of having a mind. But now, increasingly, researchers who study octopuses are convinced that these boneless, alien animals—creatures whose ancestors diverged from the lineage that would lead to ours roughly 500 to 700 million years ago—have developed intelligence, emotions, and individual personalities. Their findings are challenging our understanding of consciousness itself.

I had always longed to meet an octopus. Now was my chance: senior aquarist Scott Dowd arranged an introduction. In a back room, he would open the top of Athena's tank. If she consented, I could touch her. The heavy lid covering her tank separated our two worlds. One world was mine and yours, the reality of air and land, where we lumber through life governed by a backbone and constrained by jointed limbs and gravity. The other world was hers, the reality of a nearly gelatinous being breathing water and moving weightlessly through it. We think of our world as the "real" one, but Athena's is realer still: after all, most of the world is ocean, and most animals live there. Regardless of whether they live on land or water, more than 95 percent of all animals are invertebrates, like Athena.

The moment the lid was off, we reached for each other. She had already oozed from the far corner of her lair, where she had been hiding, to the top of the tank to investigate her visitor. Her eight arms boiled up, twisting, slippery, to meet mine. I plunged both my arms elbow deep into the fifty-seven-degree water.

Athena's melon-sized head bobbed to the surface. Her left eye (octopuses have one dominant eye like humans have a dominant hand) swiveled in its socket to meet mine. "She's looking at you," Dowd said.

As we gazed into each other's eyes, Athena encircled my arms with hers, latching on with first dozens, then hundreds of her sensitive, dexterous suckers. Each arm has more than two hundred of them. The famous naturalist and explorer William Beebe found the touch of the octopus repulsive. "I have always a struggle before I can make my hands do their duty and seize a tentacle," he confessed. But to me, Athena's suckers felt like an alien's kiss— at once a probe and a caress. Although an octopus can taste with all of its skin, in the suckers both taste and touch are exquisitely developed. Athena was tasting me and feeling me at once, knowing my skin, and possibly the blood and bone beneath, in a way I could never fathom.

When I stroked her soft head with my fingertips, she changed color beneath my touch, her ruby-flecked skin going white and smooth. This, I learned, is a sign of a relaxed octopus. An agitated giant Pacific octopus turns red, its skin gets pimply, and it erects two papillae over the eyes, which some divers say look like horns. One name for the species is "devil fish." With sharp, parrotlike beaks, octopuses can bite, and most have neurotoxic, flesh-dissolving venom. The pressure from an octopus's suckers can tear flesh (one scientist calculated that to break the hold of the suckers of the much smaller common octopus would require a quarter ton of force). One volunteer who interacted with an octopus left the aquarium with arms covered in red hickeys.

Occasionally an octopus takes a dislike to someone. One of Athena's predecessors at the aquarium, Truman, felt this way about a female volunteer. Using his funnel, the siphon near the side of the head used to jet through the sea, Truman would shoot a soaking stream of salt water at this young woman whenever he got a chance. Later, she quit her volunteer position for college. But when she returned to visit several months later, Truman, who hadn't squirted anyone in the meanwhile, took one look at her and instantly soaked her again.

Athena was remarkably gentle with me—even as she began to transfer her grip from her smaller, outer suckers to the larger ones. She seemed to be slowly but steadily pulling me into her tank. Had it been big enough to accommodate my body, I would have gone in willingly. But at this point, I asked Dowd if perhaps I should try to detach from some of the suckers. With his help, Athena and I pulled gently apart.

I was honored that she appeared comfortable with me. But what did she know about me that informed her opinion? When Athena looked into my eyes, what was she thinking?

While Alexa Warburton was researching her senior thesis at Middlebury College's newly created octopus lab, "every day," she said, "was a disaster."

She was working with two species: the California two-spot, with a head the size of a clementine, and the smaller, Florida species, *Octopus joubini*. Her objective was to study the octopuses' behavior in a T-shaped maze. But her study subjects were constantly thwarting her.

The first problem was keeping the octopuses alive. The four-hundred-gallon tank was divided into separate compartments for each animal. But even though students hammered in dividers, the octopuses found ways to dig beneath them—and eat each other. Or they'd mate, which is equally lethal. Octopuses die after mating and laying eggs, but first they go senile, acting like a person with dementia. "They swim loop-the-loop in the tank, they look all googly-eyed, they won't look you in the eye or attack prey,"

Warburton said. One senile octopus crawled out of the tank, squeezed into a crack in the wall, dried up, and died.

It seemed to Warburton that some of the octopuses were purposely uncooperative. To run the T-maze, the pre-veterinary student had to scoop an animal from its tank with a net and transfer it to a bucket. With bucket firmly covered, octopus and researcher would take the elevator down to the room with the maze. Some octopuses did not like being removed from their tanks. They would hide. They would squeeze into a corner where they couldn't be pried out. They would hold on to some object with their arms and not let go.

Some would let themselves be captured, only to use the net as a trampoline. They'd leap off the mesh and onto the floor—and then run for it. Yes, *run*. "You'd chase them under the tank, back and forth, like you were chasing a cat," Warburton said. "It's so *weird*!"

Octopuses in captivity actually escape their watery enclosures with alarming frequency. While on the move, they have been discovered on carpets, along bookshelves, in a teapot, and inside the aquarium tanks of other fish—upon whom they have usually been dining.

Even though the Middlebury octopuses were disaster prone, Warburton liked certain individuals very much. Some, she said, "would lift their arms out of the water like dogs jump up to greet you." Though in their research papers the students refer to each octopus by a number, the students named them all. One of the *joubini* was such a problem they named her The Bitch. "Catching her for the maze always took twenty minutes," Warburton said. "She'd grip on to something and not let go. Once she got stuck in a filter and we couldn't get her out. It was awful!"

Then there was Wendy. Warburton used Wendy as part of her thesis presentation, a formal event that was videotaped. First

Wendy squirted salt water at her, drenching her nice suit. Then, as Warburton tried to show how octopuses use the T-maze, Wendy scurried to the bottom of the tank and hid in the sand. Warburton says the whole debacle occurred because the octopus realized in advance what was going to happen. "Wendy," she said, "just didn't feel like being caught in the net."

Data from Warburton's experiments showed that the California two-spots quickly learned which side of a T-maze offered a terra-cotta pot to hide in. But Warburton learned far more than her experiments revealed. "Science," she says, "can only say so much. I know they watched me. I know they sometimes followed me. But they are so different from anything we normally study. How do you prove the intelligence of someone so different?"

Measuring the minds of other creatures is a perplexing problem. One yardstick scientists use is brain size, since humans have big brains. But size doesn't always match smarts. As is well known in electronics, anything can be miniaturized. Small brain size was the evidence once used to argue that birds were stupid—before some birds were proven intelligent enough to compose music, invent dance steps, ask questions, and do math.

Octopuses have the largest brains of any invertebrate. Athena's is the size of a walnut—as big as the brain of the famous African gray parrot, Alex, who learned to use more than one hundred spoken words meaningfully. That's proportionally bigger than the brains of most of the largest dinosaurs.

Another measure of intelligence: you can count neurons. The common octopus has about 130 million of them in its brain. A human has 100 billion. But this is where things get weird. Three-fifths of an octopus's neurons are not in the brain; they're in its arms.

"It is as if each arm has a mind of its own," says Peter

Godfrey-Smith, a diver, professor of philosophy at the Graduate Center of the City University of New York, and an admirer of octopuses. For example, researchers who cut off an octopus's arm (which the octopus can regrow) discovered that not only does the arm crawl away on its own, but if the arm meets a food item, it seizes it—and tries to pass it to where the mouth would be if the arm were still connected to its body.

"Meeting an octopus," writes Godfrey-Smith, "is like meeting an intelligent alien." Their intelligence sometimes even involves changing colors and shapes. One video online shows a mimic octopus alternately morphing into a flatfish, several sea snakes, and a lionfish by changing color, altering the texture of its skin, and shifting the position of its body. Another video shows an octopus materializing from a clump of algae. Its skin exactly matches the algae from which it seems to bloom—until it swims away.

For its color palette, the octopus uses three layers of three different types of cells near the skin's surface. The deepest layer passively reflects background light. The topmost may contain the colors yellow, red, brown, and black. The middle layer shows an array of glittering blues, greens, and golds. But how does an octopus decide what animal to mimic, what colors to turn? Scientists have no idea, especially given that octopuses are likely *color-blind*.

But new evidence suggests a breathtaking possibility. Woods Hole Marine Biological Laboratory and University of Washington researchers found that the skin of the cuttlefish *Sepia officinalis*, a color-changing cousin of octopuses, contains gene sequences usually expressed only in the light-sensing retina of the eye. In other words, cephalopods—octopuses, cuttlefish, and squid—may be able to see with their skin.

The American philosopher Thomas Nagel once wrote a famous paper titled "What Is It Like to Be a Bat?" Bats can see with sound. Like dolphins, they can locate their prey using echoes. Nagel concluded it was impossible to know what it's like to be a bat. And a bat is a fellow mammal like us—not someone who tastes with its suckers, sees with its skin, and whose severed arms can wander about, each with a mind of its own. Nevertheless, there are researchers still working diligently to understand what it's like to be an octopus.

Jennifer Mather spent most of her time in Bermuda floating face-down on the surface of the water at the edge of the sea. Breathing through a snorkel, she was watching *Octopus vulgaris*—the common octopus. Although indeed common (they are found in tropical and temperate waters worldwide), at the time of her study in the mid-1980s, "nobody knew what they were doing."

In a relay with other students from six-thirty in the morning till six-thirty at night, Mather worked to find out. Sometimes she'd see an octopus hunting. A hunting expedition could take five minutes or three hours. The octopus would capture something, inject it with venom, and carry it home to eat. "Home," Mather found, is where octopuses spend most of their time. A home, or den, which an octopus may occupy only a few days before switching to a new one, is a place where the shell-less octopus can safely hide: a hole in a rock, a discarded shell, or a cubbyhole in a sunken ship. One species, the Pacific red octopus, particularly likes to den in stubby, brown, glass beer bottles.

One octopus Mather was watching had just returned home and was cleaning the front of the den with its arms. Then, suddenly, it left the den, crawled a meter away, picked up one particular rock and placed the rock in front of the den. Two minutes later, the octopus ventured forth to select a second rock. Then it chose a third. Attaching suckers to all the rocks, the octopus carried the load home, slid through the den opening, and carefully arranged the three objects in front. Then it went to sleep. What the octopus was thinking seemed obvious: "Three rocks are enough. Good night!"

The scene has stayed with Mather. The octopus "must have had some concept," she said, "of what it wanted to make itself feel safe enough to go to sleep." And the octopus knew how to get what it wanted: by employing foresight, planning—and perhaps even tool use. Mather is the lead author of *Octopus: The Ocean's Intelligent Invertebrate*, which includes observations of octopuses who dismantle Lego sets and open screw-top jars. Coauthor Roland Anderson reports that octopuses even learned to open the childproof caps on Extra Strength Tylenol pill bottles—a feat that eludes many humans with university degrees.

In another experiment, Anderson gave octopuses plastic pill bottles painted different shades and with different textures to see which evoked more interest. Usually each octopus would grasp a bottle to see if it were edible and then cast it off. But to his astonishment, Anderson saw one of the octopuses doing something striking: she was blowing carefully modulated jets of water from her funnel to send the bottle to the other end of her aquarium where the water flow sent it back to her. She repeated the action twenty times. By the eighteenth time, Anderson was already on the phone with Mather with the news: "She's bouncing the ball!"

This octopus wasn't the only one to use the bottle as a toy. Another octopus in the study also shot water at the bottle, sending it back and forth across the water's surface, rather than circling the tank. Anderson's observations were reported in the *Journal of Comparative Psychology*. "This fit all the criteria for play behavior," said Anderson. "Only intelligent animals play—animals like crows and chimps, dogs and humans."

Aquarists who care for octopuses feel that not only can these animals play with toys, but they may *need* to play with toys. An *Octopus Enrichment Handbook* has been developed by Cincinnati's Newport Aquarium, with ideas of how to keep these creatures entertained. One suggestion is to hide food inside Mr. Potato Head and let your octopus dismantle it. At the Seattle Aquarium, giant Pacific octopuses play with a baseball-sized plastic ball that can be screwed together by twisting the two halves. Sometimes the mollusks screw the halves back together after eating the prey inside.

At the New England Aquarium, it took an engineer who worked on the design of cubic zirconium to devise a puzzle worthy of a brain like Athena's. Wilson Menashi, who began volunteering at the aquarium weekly after retiring from the Arthur D. Little Corporation sixteen years ago, devised a series of three Plexiglas cubes, each with a different latch. The smallest cube has a sliding latch that twists to lock down, like the bolt on a horse stall. Aquarist Bill Murphy puts a crab inside the clear cube and leaves the lid open. Later he lets the octopus lift open the lid. Finally he locks the lid, and invariably the octopus figures out how to open it.

Next he locks the first cube within a second one. The new latch slides counterclockwise to catch on a bracket. The third box is the largest, with two different locks: a bolt that slides into position to lock down, and a second one like a lever arm, sealing the lid much like the top of an old-fashioned glass canning jar.

All the octopuses Murphy has known learned fast. They typically master a box within two or three once-a-week tries. "Once they 'get it,' " he says, "they can open it very fast"—within three or four minutes. But each may use a different strategy.

George, a calm octopus, opened the boxes methodically. The impetuous Gwenevere squeezed the second-largest box so hard she broke it, leaving a hole two inches wide. Truman, Murphy said, was "an opportunist." One day, inside the smaller of the two boxes, Murphy put two crabs, who started to fight. Truman was too excited to bother with locks. He poured his seven-foot-long body through the two-inch crack Gwenevere had made, and visitors looked into his exhibit to find the giant octopus squeezed, suckers flattened, into the tiny space between the walls of the fourteen-cubic-inch box outside and the six-cubic-inch one inside it. Truman stayed inside half an hour. He never opened the inner box—probably he was too cramped.

Three weeks after I had first met Athena, I returned to the aquarium to meet the man who had designed the cubes. Menashi, a quiet grandfather with a dark moustache, volunteers every Tuesday. "He has a real way with octopuses," Dowd and Murphy told me. I was eager to see how Athena behaved with him.

Murphy opened the lid of her tank, and Athena rose to the surface eagerly. A bucket with a handful of fish sat nearby. Did she rise so eagerly sensing the food? Or was it the sight of her friend that attracted her? "She knows me," Menashi answered softly.

Anderson's experiments with giant Pacific octopuses in Seattle prove Menashi is right. The study exposed eight octopuses to two unfamiliar humans, dressed identically in blue aquarium shirts. One person consistently fed a particular octopus, and another always touched it with a bristly stick. Within a week, at first sight of the people, most octopuses moved toward the feeders and away from the irritators, at whom they occasionally aimed their water-shooting funnels.

Upon seeing Menashi, Athena reached up gently and grasped his hands and arms. She flipped upside down, and he placed a capelin in some of the suckers near her mouth, at the center of her arms. The fish vanished. After she had eaten, Athena floated in the tank upside down, like a puppy asking for a belly rub. Her arms twisted lazily. I took one in my hand to feel the suckers— did that arm know it had hold of a different person than the other arms did? Her grip felt calm, relaxed. With me, earlier, she seemed playful, exploratory, excited. The way she held Menashi with her suckers seemed to me like the way a long-married couple holds hands at the movies.

I leaned over the tank to look again into her eyes, and she bobbed up to return my gaze. "She has eyelids like a person does," Menashi said. He gently slid his hand near one of her eyes, causing her to slowly wink.

Biologists have long noted the similarities between the eyes of an octopus and the eyes of a human. Canadian zoologist N. J. Berrill called it "the single most startling feature of the whole animal kingdom" that these organs are nearly identical: both animals' eyes have transparent corneas, regulate light with iris diaphragms, and focus lenses with a ring of muscle.

Scientists are currently debating whether we and octopuses evolved eyes separately, or whether a common ancestor had the makings of the eye. But intelligence is another matter. "The same thing that got them their smarts isn't the same thing that got us our smarts," says Mather, "because our two ancestors didn't *have* any smarts." Half a billion years ago, the brainiest thing on the planet had only a few neurons. Octopus and human intelligence evolved independently.

"Octopuses," writes philosopher Godfrey-Smith, "are a separate experiment in the evolution of the mind." And that, he feels, is what makes the study of the octopus mind so philosophically interesting.

The octopus mind and the human mind probably evolved for different reasons. Humans—like other vertebrates whose intelligence we recognize (parrots, elephants, and whales)—are long-lived, social beings. Most scientists agree that an important event that drove the flowering of our intelligence was when our ancestors began to live in social groups. Decoding and developing the many subtle relationships among our fellows, and keeping track of these changing relationships over the course of the many decades of a typical human lifespan, was surely a major force shaping our minds.

But octopuses are neither long-lived nor social. Athena, to my sorrow, may live only a few more months—the natural lifespan of a giant Pacific octopus is only three years. If the aquarium added another octopus to her tank, one might eat the other. Except to mate, most octopuses have little to do with others of their kind.

So why is the octopus so intelligent? What is its mind *for*? Mather thinks she has the answer. She believes the event driving the octopus toward intelligence was the loss of the ancestral shell. Losing the shell freed the octopus for mobility. Now they didn't need to wait for food to find them; they could hunt like tigers. And while most octopuses love crab best, they hunt and eat dozens of other species—each of which demands a different hunting strategy. Each animal you hunt may demand a different skill set: Will you camouflage yourself for a stalk-and-ambush attack? Shoot through the sea for a fast chase? Or crawl out of the water to capture escaping prey?

Losing the protective shell was a trade-off. Just about anything big enough to eat an octopus will do so. Each species of predator also demands a different evasion strategy—from flashing warning coloration if your attacker is vulnerable to venom, to changing color and shape to camouflage, to fortifying the door to your home with rocks.

Such intelligence is not always evident in the laboratory. "In the lab, you give the animals this situation, and they react," points out Mather. But in the wild, "the octopus is actively discovering his environment, not waiting for it to hit him. The animal makes the decision to go out and get information, figures out how to get the information, gathers it, uses it, stores it. This has a great deal to do with consciousness."

So what does it feel like to be an octopus? Philosopher Godfrey-Smith has given this a great deal of thought, especially when he meets octopuses and their relatives, giant cuttlefish, on dives in his native Australia. "They come forward and look at you. They reach out to touch you with their arms," he said. "It's remarkable how little is known about them . . . but I could see it turning out that we have to change the way we think of the nature of the mind itself to take into account minds with less of a centralized self."

"I think consciousness comes in different flavors," agrees Mather. "Some may have consciousness in a way we may not be able to imagine."

In May, I visited Athena a third time. I wanted to see if she recognized me. But how could I tell? Scott Dowd opened the top of her tank for me. Athena had been in a back corner but floated immediately to the top, arms outstretched, upside down.

This time I offered her only one arm. I had injured a knee and, feeling wobbly, used my right hand to steady me while I stood on the stool to lean over the tank. Athena in turn gripped me with only one of her arms, and very few of her suckers. Her hold on me was remarkably gentle.

I was struck by this, since Murphy and others had first described Athena's personality to me as "feisty." "They earn their names," Murphy had told me. Athena is named for the Greek goddess of wisdom, war, and strategy. She is not usually a laid-back octopus, like George had been. "Athena could pull you into the tank," Murphy had warned. "She's curious about what you are."

Was she less curious now? Did she remember me? I was disappointed that she did not bob her head up to look at me. But perhaps she didn't need to. She may have known from the taste of my skin who I was. But why was this feisty octopus hanging in front of me in the water, upside down?

Then I thought I might know what she wanted from me. She was begging. Dowd asked around and learned that Athena hadn't eaten in a couple of days, then allowed me the thrilling privilege of handing her a capelin.

Perhaps I had understood something basic about what it felt like to be Athena at that moment: she was hungry. I handed a fish to one of her larger suckers, and she began to move it toward her mouth. But soon she brought more arms to the task, and covered the fish with many suckers—as if she were licking her fingers, savoring the meal.

A week after I last visited Athena, I was shocked to receive this e-mail from Scott Dowd: "Sorry to write with some sad news. Athena appears to be in her final days, or even hours. She will live on, though, through your conveyance." Later that same day, Dowd wrote to tell me that she had died. To my surprise, I found myself in tears.

Why such sorrow? I had understood from the start that octopuses don't live very long. I also knew that while Athena did seem to recognize me, I was not by any means her special friend. But she was very significant to me, both as an individual and as a representative from her octopodan world. She had given me a great gift: a deeper understanding of what it means to think, to feel, and to know. I was eager to meet more of her kind.

And so, it was with some excitement that I read this e-mail from Dowd a few weeks later: "There is a young pup octopus headed to Boston from the Pacific Northwest. Come shake hands (x8) when you can."

FRANCESCA ARAN MURPHY

Oriental Aspects of Occidental Faith

FROM *First Things*

IN MY FIFTEEN YEARS IN ABERDEEN, THE OLD ABERDEEN MOSQUE went from a tiny to a flourishing enterprise, with Muslim men overflowing the building onto the surrounding streets. Between 1995 and 2010 in northeast Scotland, the sight of women in burqas and niqabs went from rare to commonplace. The number of ethnic supermarkets serving halal lamb and venison quadrupled. Notably, some of the women clustering with their prams round the Old Aberdeen mosque were evidently not immigrants or from immigrant families. Islam is on the rise in Britain, both by the influx of immigrants and, increasingly, through the winning of converts.

A recent Pew Forum report estimated that the number of British Muslims has almost doubled in the last decade, from 1.6 million in 2001 to 2.9 million today. One study estimated that five thousand Britons a year choose to become Muslim. Why, asks the journalist Melanie McDonagh in *The Spectator*, "is it that young folk revolted by contemporary excess don't simply make for the local C of E or Catholic church and rediscover the religion of their grandmothers, rather than getting their spirituality via

Islam?" Her answer is robustly Chestertonian: "It is the notion that what exists abroad, or what is foreign to your own background, is somehow superior to what you've grown up with, what's under your nose."

Attraction to what once would have been called Oriental religion, Chesterton insisted, comes not from an excess, but from a failure of imagination. It takes real imagination, he asserted, to see the homely and familiar, or what our grandmothers taught us, as redolent with wondrous, religious appeal. That was true of those of Chesterton's contemporaries who went for "Madame Blavatsky religion," pseudo-Buddhism, and the cornucopia of fake orientalisms generated by the British Raj.

This attraction to the exotic was found even in the Victorian working class. Stationed in Palestine during the First World War, my grandfather was so bowled over by the sight of hooded and kaftaned Middle Eastern men that he lost his Christian faith. This eighteen-year-old boy thought anyone who swirled out of the desert dressed like that claiming to be the Son of God could easily, and mistakenly, have been believed. Like many Englishmen of his time and class he owned a copy of T. E. Lawrence's *Seven Pillars of Wisdom*. His love for the Orient was a typically distant one: He left English soil twice, once for what he called "the Great War" and again in the 1970s, when he embarrassed his daughter by telling each French waitress he met, in English, about the circumstances of his previous visit to their country.

Today no British person could encounter Islam as such exotic souvenir territory. The curry takeaway, with its Muslim proprietor, is precisely what is under their nose. The Old Aberdonian Scots who wait patiently, and always respectfully, for business to resume in The Khyber Pass, once the owners have finished eating for the first time that day, know much more about Ramadan than they do about Lent.

. . .

Twenty minutes away from genteel Old Aberdeen, with its medieval university, mosque, and Khyber Pass, lies Tillydrone, a drug-infested working-class district. I spent time there last summer, searching for a delinquent cat. Its only public building that I did not tack with a "reward" photo of Pius was the local church, since it was always locked. If it had been Episcopalian or Catholic, rather than Church of Scotland, it would likewise have been locked against vandals. The mosque in Old Aberdeen is locked, too, out of hours.

Walking between the two communities made me think that if I was a working-class teenage girl with any sense, I'd consider picking a mate from the boys outside the mosque. There are decent people in Tillydrone, and families, one of which returned the miscreant animal. But they receive no apparent moral sustenance from corporate religion. Even wearing a burqa might be a small price to pay for religious leaders who insist the males take on the responsibility of being breadwinners.

Churches look like places where weddings happen, but not where marriages hold together. Those burqaed women with their prams are an obvious expression of the culture of the mosque. The churches don't feel like communities in the same way. McDonagh notes that "many girls who convert to Islam do so because their boyfriends/future husbands are Muslims." She doesn't ask why they chose Muslims as boyfriends, and the "appeal of the exotic" doesn't speak to the question in contemporary Britain.

Unlike the Ramadan-observant Muslims, Catholics replaced their socially binding meatless Fridays and Lents with amorphous good intentions about "giving something up." So-called intentional Christianity has a middle-class, intellectual appeal, but adopting it has cost the churches the working class. I was reminded of this while looking with an Irish Dominican friend at a magazine photo of thousands of Muslims at prayer. He commented that we had lost the habit of repetitive prayer. The rosary, he said, is how less-educated people like to pray. McDonagh notes that many of the new Muslims in London are West Indian youths, "for whom Islam offers greater discipline and certainty than the Pentecostalism of their parents."

She doesn't ask whether that applies equally to the current practice of Catholicism and Anglicanism. Ramadan might make more sense to the literal-minded than giving something up. When I told an Indian shopkeeper I was buying his beans for a vegetarian Friday dinner-party, he said, "Very few Christians here keep their faith." That might not be true, but it is true that Christian practices are less tangible than Islamic ones. And so the recent decision of the Catholic bishops of England and Wales to bring back the traditional Friday fast presents an evangelistic opportunity. For the Friday fast, like Ramadan and similar disciplines, carries its own visible apologetic.

To a Christian not much more knowledgeable about it than Chesterton was, Islam seems like the perfect "political religion"— almost, one could say, the perfect "Marxist" religion. A system of rewards and punishments in the afterlife correlates with a highly moralized and cohesive system of social organization on earth. Everyone knows, and some will even acknowledge, that British Islam also has a much darker side. Former home secretary Jack Straw's recent observation, corroborated by interviews on a Radio 4 program, that many Pakistani boys see English girls as "easy meat" shows us what it is. That sensible teenager who selects a Muslim mate had better know that an imam who encourages boys to marry and reproduce will discreetly avert his gaze when the husband mistreats his wife. Just "imitating Islam" is not an answer to Christianity's current failures in Europe.

. . .

If British Christianity ever regains the habits it once had, of specified culinary abstinence, repetitive prayer, and chaste fertility, it won't be in imitation of Islam, but it might be as a recovery of its own originally "Oriental" element. Outside the imams, Islam has no clerical hierarchy. The horizontality of its communal prayer is a precise visual expression of the core concept of brotherhood in Islam.

Christians fast together in recognition of their solidarity in the body of the crucified Christ. This understanding of solidarity is, if anything, more Oriental than the more straightforward Muslim conception of brotherhood, which seems by comparison rather "Latin" and rational. Christian repetitive prayer, like the rosary, is a means of mental absorption in the historical mysteries of the life of Christ. It's like yoga, but more Eastern than that.

Likewise, the Christian, Pauline image of marriage, in which a man and wife become "one body" like the body of Christ, smacks of the *Arabian Nights,* in contrast to the more legal conception of marriage, which legitimates divorce within Islam. Or perhaps that is just my grandfather talking, about how Christianity could make converts in Britain today.

DAVID NOVAK

The Man-made Messiah

FROM *First Things*

THE MOST RECOGNIZED FACE OF ANY JEWISH LEADER OF THE past fifty years belongs to the late Rabbi Menachem Mendel Schneerson, even more so today than at his death in 1994. There are few Jews who have not seen the picture of the Lubavitcher rebbe on billboards or in other media or who have not encountered one of his many "representatives," young men and women who have dedicated their lives to the dissemination of his teachings. At the core of those teachings is a messianic theology that is emphasized in varying degrees by his Chabad emissaries, even more so posthumously than during his lifetime. *Chabad* is the generic name of the Hasidic community he led for forty-four years; *Lubavitch* is the name of the town in Belarus where the Chabad community was centered before the First World War.

This messianism doubtless fires Chabad's missionary fervor. It distinguishes Chabad from more insular Hasidic communities and motivates Chabad to employ the same techniques of modern publicity as do Christian and Islamic missionary movements. The thrust of this messianic theology is the strong suggestion that Rabbi Schneerson himself is the Messiah-King, thus making the essential task of his representatives (called *shluchim* in Hebrew) to prepare the Jewish people, and along with them all humankind, to affirm that kingship.

The Lubavitcher rebbe—the name used by those who do not consider him to be "*the* Rebbe"—is the subject of two important new books: the more biographical *The Rebbe: The Life and Afterlife of Menachem Mendel Schneerson* by Professors Samuel Heilman and Menachem Friedman, and the more theoretical *Open Secret: Postmessianic Messianism and the Mystical Revision of Menachem Mendel Schneerson* by Professor Elliot Wolfson. But before turning to the controversy these volumes have occasioned, we need to understand *what* a Hasidic rebbe does, to make clear what kind of Hasidic rebbe was Menachem Mendel Schneerson. We must also understand the meaning of the messianic claims made by him or by his followers and consider the future of a community now living his "afterlife."

Traditional Jewish communities are led by a rabbi of recognized authority (a *rav* in Hebrew). A traditional rabbi is the man to whom the community and its members turn to rule on what Jewish law requires of them, particularly in cases of doubt. The rabbi is often the regular preacher in the synagogue, the man whose sermons offer his community more general theological and moral guidance. But a Hasidic rebbe is much more than a rabbinical jurist and preacher, although some of them also have functioned in these roles. Heilman and Friedman accurately describe a rebbe as "an intermediary between his followers and the Almighty, capable of bestowing blessings as well as transmitting the will of God." As such, this is the man (although there once was a woman who functioned as a rebbe) who makes those policies of a Hasidic community that seem to need more than ordinary legal or theological justifications or who can get a new commandment ad hoc directly from God. That is why individual Hasidim come to their rebbe for divine direction in life dilemmas with no simple legal or theological solution. In fact, in most Hasidic communities, quotidian legal and theological tasks are usually assigned to a rebbe's rabbinical subordinates.

To compare with Catholicism, one could say an ordinary rabbi functions like a canon lawyer or an official theologian, whereas a rebbe bears a charismatic spiritual authority more comparable to that of a pope. Yet just as a pope claims only to be Christ's vicar, not Christ himself, so does a Hasidic rebbe not normally claim to be the Messiah. That is what made Menachem Mendel Schneerson a very different kind of rebbe. And Rabbi Schneerson's own not so subtle suggestions that he himself might be the Messiah mean that his more "messianic" followers are not simply inventing his messiahhood out of their own collective imagination. Indeed, as Wolfson's study shows, this messianic preoccupation has been a central feature of Chabad theology from its beginnings in the works of Rabbi Shneur Zalman of Lyady, the founder of Chabad Hasidism. This type of messianism also prompted Professor David Berger of Yeshiva University to write his controversial 2001 book *The Rebbe, the Messiah, and the Scandal of Orthodox Indifference*, in which he argues that the similarities of Chabad messianic theology to Christology make it heretical, if not outright apostasy from Judaism.

As Heilman and Friedman tell the story, the future Rebbe was born Menachem Mendel in 1902 to distant relatives of the Lubavitcher rebbe, Shalom Ber Schneerson. In the dynastic succession typical of Hasidic rebbes, Shalom Ber Schneerson was succeeded on his death by his son, Yosef Yitzchak, born in 1880. In 1928 Menachem Mendel became Rabbi Yosef Yitzchak Schneerson's son-in-law and took on his last name. Between 1928 and 1941 (the year he arrived in the United States), Menachem

Mendel Schneerson and his wife lived first in Berlin and then in Paris, where he studied and tried to practice engineering though remaining dependent on his father-in-law for financial support. Although they kept close ties to the Lubavitch community, it seems the young Schneerson couple planned a more independent life for themselves. (Even after Menachem Schneerson became the Lubavitcher rebbe in 1950, his wife, Moussia, continued to live her own rather private life and insisted on being called "Mrs. Schneerson" rather than "the Lubavitcher *rebbetzin*," or "rebbe's wife.") The fall of France to the Nazis forced the Schneersons to follow Rabbi Yosef Yitzchak to the United States, where the Lubavitcher community had established its headquarters in the Crown Heights section of Brooklyn.

In New York, Rabbi Schneerson became more involved in the leadership of the Lubavitch community, especially as his father-in-law became more infirm. On Yosef Yitzchak's death in 1950, the patrilineal succession common in the Hasidic world was excluded, as the sixth Lubavitcher rebbe had only daughters. The big question among Lubavitchers—and among other interested parties in the Hasidic world and the world of the ultraorthodox yeshivas—was "Who will Yosef Yitzchak's successor be?" His oldest daughter, Chana, was married to Rabbi Abraham Gourary, who acted as the rebbe's executive secretary. But, as Heilman and Friedman put it, "Gourary . . . appeared to many people to lack personal charisma"—unlike Menachem Mendel Schneerson. After a brief struggle for succession, the Lubavitcher Hasidim chose Menachem Mendel Schneerson to be their seventh rebbe, and Rabbi Gourary and most of his supporters fell into line.

Before the seventh rebbe's succession in 1950, Lubavitch did not stand out from its larger and more influential rivals, such as Satmar, Ger, and Belz. The power and vision of Menachem Mendel Schneerson's leadership quickly changed that. On several key theological and political issues, he reversed the usual Hasidic turn inward into a new kind of outreach. He sought not only to bring Chabad Hasidism into a radically new world but, even more, to bring that new world to Chabad. Some saw this as Lubavitch's adjustment to the new world, but Lubavitchers themselves see this as Chabad's turning that new world toward its own truth.

The issues on which Rabbi Menachem Mendel Schneerson made a big difference—at least in the larger Orthodox world—concern nonreligious Jews, non-Jews, and the state of Israel. All of this is explained well in the Heilman-Friedman biography, and some of it in Wolfson's study of Rabbi Schneerson's theology.

To the leaders of East European Orthodox Jewish communities before the Second World War, America was a *treifah medinah*—a "nonkosher domain"—a place where Jews were pulled into a vortex of vulgar materialism and a culture that quickly and thoroughly melted down traditional Jewish devotion to the Torah and the practice of its commandments. This attitude was especially prevalent among the Hasidic rebbes, who advocated the most thorough Jewish separation possible. In their eyes, the dangers to Jewish bodies posed by East European societies were to be preferred to the danger to Jewish souls posed by American society and (in the rebbes' eyes) its atheistic culture. That is why few Hasidim, and even fewer Lubavitcher Hasidim, settled in America until after the Second World War. And that is certainly how Yosef Yitzchak Schneerson felt about America, even after he took refuge there in 1940, following his release from a Soviet prison. On his succession, Menachem Mendel Schneerson proposed a radically different view of America and the role it could play in Jewish revival.

Most Hasidic rebbes kept their followers away from the great majority of secularized or vaguely religious American Jews. By the end of his life, the man whom Lubavitcher Hasidim now call "the previous rebbe," Yosef Yitzchak Schneerson, was beginning to send out some of his disciples to try to bring more Judaism to these "lost" Jews. In the past, the only type of outreach to other Jews practiced by Lubavitch or any other Hasidic community was to attract the followers of other Hasidic rebbes or other Orthodox Jews (usually from the anti-Hasidic yeshiva world) to become the Hasidim of their rebbe. When, in 1949, Yosef Yitzchak Schneerson sent some of his disciples to encourage more Jewish religious observance at the decidedly secular Brandeis University, he signaled a departure from Hasidic and even Lubavitch precedents. Yosef Yitzchak Schneerson saw the Jews of America as unlike the European Jews who knew the traditional Judaism they had willingly deserted. He characterized American Jews as the "kidnapped child" of whom the Talmud speaks: a person who did not desert Judaism but whom the traditional Jewish community had never known at all. "Returning" these people to the Jewish fold did not entail winning them back to a tradition they had rejected. Instead, they were to be introduced to Jewish identity for the first time.

When Menachem Mendel Schneerson became the Lubavitcher rebbe, he expanded this outreach. He intoned in his writings and speeches that this outreach was necessary to bring about the arrival of the Messiah. Chabad outreach did not recognize Jewish secularism or what Rabbi Schneerson considered to be the compromised Judaism of Reform and Conservative Jews. Chabad looked at these Jews only as lost individuals. For Rabbi Menachem Mendel Schneerson, anything less than Jewish Orthodoxy (meaning full acceptance of the divinely revealed Torah and the authority of Jewish legal tradition, Halakhah) was not Judaism at all; indeed, even non-Hasidic Orthodox Jews—and even non-Lubavitch Hasidim—could find the truest and fullest form of Judaism only in Chabad. As Heilman and Friedman report, Rabbi Schneerson's emissaries "would act as agents provocateurs, people who *seemed* open to modernity and America, but only in order to change it."

But Rabbi Schneerson's departure from traditional suspicion of America went deeper. He understood that America had not only a different kind of Jew but also a different kind of Gentile. Despite a residual anti-Semitism, Americans on the whole not only are friendlier to Jews but also have a greater respect for Judaism. Unlike many Orthodox Jews today, who view with suspicion American Christian support for Israel and other Jewish causes, the Lubavitcher rebbe saw the underlying affinity: American Christianity is steeped in the Bible. And America itself, if not in an official political sense, is still very much a Christian country culturally. American Christianity, moreover, retains the influence of Puritan Calvinism, which, more than any other Christian current, emphasized the Old Testament.

What is the practical import of American biblicism? One can see the Bible teaching two main truths, one universal and the other particular. The universal truth is that there are certain moral norms whose affirmation can be expected of all human beings. This is what the rabbinic tradition called the "Noahide commandments," Noah being the progenitor of all humankind after the Flood. The sign of a truly decent society, one that Jews can respect and even participate in, is the seriousness with which that society takes these universal norms, whatever they might be called.

The particular truth taught in the Bible is that the Jewish people are the elect of God and play a unique role in God's ultimate redemption of the world from sin and death. A good non-Jewish society (or civilization) is one that takes the Noahide laws seriously and recognizes the ultimate importance of having Jews teaching and practicing a flourishing Judaism in its midst. Rabbi

Schneerson judged America to be such a society—a society in which both the universal and particular teaching of the Bible are taken seriously.

The political effects of this type of theological speculation about America came to the fore relatively early in Rabbi Schneerson's career as the Lubavitcher rebbe. In 1962, when the largely secularist leaders of American Jewry were vigorously fighting the recitation of any prayer, no matter how "nonsectarian," in public schools, Rabbi Schneerson, in what became his first real appearance on the larger American Jewish stage, argued the opposite. After all, if there is a Noahide commandment that prohibits idolatry (the worship of "other gods"), doesn't that imply that the worship of the One God—whom all the proposed public-school prayers explicitly invoked—is required of all human beings, especially if the One God is the creator of heaven and earth represented in the Bible?

Also in the 1960s, when the leaders of American Jewry were vigorously fighting religious displays such as Christmas crèches in what Father Richard John Neuhaus called "the naked public square," Rabbi Schneerson directed his representatives to erect Hanukkah menorahs in public places wherever they could do so. To my knowledge, the only opposition to this project the Lubavitchers have encountered has been from secularist Jews who seem to be uncomfortable with anyone's religion, even their own or that of their ancestors, occupying a public space. Moreover, the choice of this particular Jewish object for public display is significant because the Hanukkah menorah is meant to proclaim to the world that God miraculously saved the Jewish people from losing their religious identity to a foreign power and its culture in the days of the Maccabees. The story appeals to the deepest levels of American identity—an archetypal identity forged by the Pilgrims at Plymouth, who risked everything to worship God publicly in their own way. Despite their quaint dress, young Lubavitchers erecting Hanukkah menorahs in the public square recall the Pilgrim Fathers, as several American Christians have told me. Indeed, they seem more American than the Jewish and Gentile secularists who want to put religion into the closet.

Nevertheless, as Wolfson reports, Rabbi Schneerson was no universalist, although he held a higher view of Gentiles, especially American Christians, than did most other Hasidic thinkers past and present. He propounded the Hasidic view, drawn from Kabbalah, that an ontological divide separates Jews from Gentiles: Jews are taken to be a distinct species, with a superior relationship with God. And that is not only because Jews are the recipients of the Sinaitic revelation (which, after all, Gentiles can access in some fashion) but also because Jews, in both soul and body, were created to be more elevated than the rest of creation and humankind. Accordingly, non-Jews are valued insofar as they respect Judaism and maintain the kind of moral society in which Jewish religion can survive and flourish.

When modern political Zionism emerged around the turn of the twentieth century, most Orthodox Jews opposed it. For most early Zionists, Zionism seemed not to be an expression of Jewish religion but rather a substitute for it. Almost all the Hasidic rebbes abhorred Zionism, including the fifth and sixth Lubavitcher rebbes, Shalom Ber Schneerson and his son and successor, Yosef Yitzchak Schneerson. They saw Zionism as yet another snare set by heretical Jewish modernity for traditional Jews. Yosef Yitzchak Schneerson persisted in this stance until the end of his life. Chabad's attitude began to change when Menachem Mendel Schneerson became the Lubavitcher rebbe in 1950, just two years after the reestablishment of the state of Israel.

Why the change in attitude—what Heilman and Friedman call "reinvention"? It could be said that Rabbi Schneerson saw the realization of the Zionist ideal in the state of Israel's presence in the contemporary world just as he saw America as the realization of the religious ideals of its Founders. Despite the secularist dangers, the state of Israel, with its Jewish majority population, offered Chabad a field for future development. Zionism was no longer an enemy, as it was in the continuing view of Chabad's archrivals, the Satmar Hasidim. On the contrary, Chabad's support of Israel and, in particular, its foreign policy has been very successful in Israel, despite a theology that denies explicit support for any secular state, even a Jewish one. Rabbi Schneerson's portrait is displayed throughout Israel without a caption because he is universally recognized. Chabad "emissaries" are everywhere, from airports to shopping centers.

While granting Rabbi Schneerson's extraordinary achievements and influence on contemporary Jewish life, traditional Judaism cannot accept the view of some of his followers that Menachem Mendel Schneerson was the Messiah. The Messiah is assumed to be a particular human being who is to perform certain acts that identify him as such. Even in the less apocalyptic type of Jewish messianism, the Messiah is still expected to gather all Israel into the land of Israel, rebuild the Temple in Jerusalem, and establish an optimal polity having strong international influence. If not supernatural, these criteria are nonetheless utopian. And according to these criteria Rabbi Menachem Mendel Schneerson cannot be the Messiah yet to come.

Elliot Wolfson offers a convoluted postmodern argument that Schneerson somehow still represented the Messiah impersonally or "transpersonally." This detracts from the creditable scholarship Wolfson applies to analyzing the vast body of Chabad writings and putting it into the overall context of the kabbalistic theology he knows so well. Heilman and Friedman, on the other hand, mar an otherwise strong narrative by indulging in shallow psychologizing and ascribing to the Lubavitcher rebbe all sorts of motives that only he and God could possibly know he ever had.

Lastly, though, the questions raised by the two Orthodox sociologists who know a good deal of the history of Hasidism are most pertinent. What, Heilman and Friedman ask, will happen to Chabad, with its now deceased rebbe whom no one outside of Chabad's own messianic circle claims to be the Messiah? They conclude, "One needs to wait at least two generations to begin to see how religious change develops and whether movements die, fractionalize, or are sustained." Yet, here and now, one can hope.

As a traditional Jew I have benefited personally from the hospitality of Chabad Hasidim on many occasions, and I marvel at how many Jews Chabad has brought back to their primordial home. That is why I hope Chabad will be sustained and will flourish. I hope the explicitly messianic Chabad Hasidim eventually will return to normative Judaism, something that has happened before to what we might call "premature" Jewish messianic movements. And I dare hope that sooner or later Chabad will choose an eighth Lubavitcher rebbe who will be a worthy successor to Menachem Mendel Schneerson and will carry forth his legacy as Menachem Mendel carried forth the legacy of his father-in-law Yosef Yitzchak. And may the Messiah come soon in our days, to validate their great efforts to bring the Jewish people, and with them all humankind, forward to God in a way no eye but God's has yet seen.

P. J. O'ROURKE

God's Engineer

FROM *The Atlantic*

WHAT IS ADMIRED AS WHIMSY COULD BE AWFUL AS FACT—REAL slithy toves in an actual wabe. The shapes of 21st-century architecture are increasingly whimsical. (Two words—*Frank Gehry*—suffice to describe the trend.) I've been looking at flighty modern buildings in Los Angeles, Shanghai, London, and Dubai. They put me in mind of the Barcelona architect of a hundred years ago, Antoni Gaudí. And they remind me why, although I am entranced by Gaudí's work, I've always been reluctant to go see it. Finally I give in. Maybe an inspection of Gaudí will help me understand the new oddball global cityscapes.

The exemplarily fantastical Casa Batlló, from 1906, is a six-story townhouse on Passeig de Gràcia, which is very much Barcelona's Park Avenue. The roof is an ocean swell thickly rippled with ceramic tiles that undulate in colors as well as curves. Vertical waves, gentle rollers, shape a facade encrusted with the mosaic technique Gaudí developed, *trencadís*. Hundreds of thousands of bright bits of china and glass are splayed in clumps and bunches: flotsam and jetsam (or a bad sun rash) as ornament. Interspersed in the *trencadís*, decorating the decor, is a picnic litter of plates splashed in motley glazes. Columns on the lower floors are modeled on human bones. Each props open a whale-jaw rictus of cast concrete. The upper-floor balconies are sheet metal hammered into pelvic girdles with strips of twisted steel like seaweed fluttering from each hip. The effect should be Casa Davy Jones's Locker. But Casa Batlló is beautiful. And it fits right into the neighborhood. Only a genius could have pulled this off.

Once in, I want to move in—aspirationally and kinetically. The hall streams. The stairs surge. There are no edges, no corners. Walls glide into ceilings. Rooms flow into rooms. It is a peristalsis house. But light, cheer, air, and comfortable proportions are everyplace. The design is meant fully for people and, what with all the tourists, is full of them. They are in good spirits, as the spirit of the house demands. Every detail is crafted to delight. Even the air shaft is a masterpiece, tiled in shades of azure, deep-tinted at the top and gradually lightening to spread sun evenly to all floors.

Three blocks up Passeig de Gràcia, Casa Milà, completed in 1910, is better yet. The big apartment building has the hard but fluid segmented continuity of an invertebrate, though its limestone shell is really supported on the kind of steel skeleton introduced not long before by Chicago architect William Le Baron Jenney. Casa Milà insinuates itself into its corner lot with a lovely dead-bleached-insect grace. Some 150 windows, all seemingly different, are arranged in sinuous asymmetry. Some are armed at their sills with ferocious railings of wrought iron that, to me, seem abstractions of mandibles, tentacles, stingers, and jellyfish sacs. The roof is separately aggressive, a banked and mounded parapet with dormer windows that could serve as embrasures, and chimneys molded to evoke Catalan knights in armor.

Casa Milà is a carapace, a fortress, but a fortress of domestic pleasantry. The apartments wander through the complexity of the building's form, so their floor plans look insane. But Gaudí didn't like blueprints or even renderings. He preferred to work from models. And the apartments are models of open-plan living, lofts in advance of fashion, except with better natural light, greater ventilation, more common sense, and a happier mood. Few lofts today have a sewing room, and none have ceiling plaster whipped like meringue.

All of Gaudí's works, however outwardly unruly, proceed from internal discipline. His father was a boilermaker. Gaudí loved geometry. To determine the catenary curves of arches, he would tack a sketch of a foundation plan on the ceiling, hang loops of string, and attach weights along the loops in proportion to down forces. Then he'd take a photograph, turn the print upside-down, and get his elevation view. Gaudí pioneered the parabolic arch, with its perfect distribution of load. The arches beneath Casa Milà's stone roof are so strong, each is built with a single course of upended bricks.

Gaudí also had a sense of proportion. Every design is sized to the effect intended. Casa Milà, for example, should be scary. But it's too human in scope and scale. It's charming instead, like a child's drawing of something scary—if your child were Degas.

Less than a mile northeast of Casa Milà is La Sagrada Família (Holy Family) basilica, where Gaudí was operating on a scale that's superhuman. He began work on the church in 1883, when he was 31. From 1914 until his death in 1926, he devoted himself solely to the project, which is still under construction and maybe always will be.

I stare with an exalted crick in my neck at the immensities of the bell towers, swirled spires of lace made from rock. (Eventually there will be 18 of them.) It would shake the faith back into anyone to look at Gaudí's depiction of all creation melting in love on the Nativity facade. I behold, with strained peripheral vision, the nave and aisles that hold 14,000 worshippers. And these are the least interesting parts of the building.

Gaudí considered the Gothic style imperfect, because buttresses are needed to hold up the soaring magnificence. The house of God should stand on its own. Gaudí found solutions in plant and animal forms, in hyperboloids, paraboloids, and helicoids (respectively, saddle-shaped curves, cones, and spirals). And he made use of fractals, structures that split into smaller replications of themselves, the way broccoli does.

Gone are the buttresses. Gothic gloom is dispelled. The sun shines through the walls from floor to roof, and through the roof as well. Genesis 1:3, ". . . and there was light."

If a Gothic cathedral is (as some have said, misapplying their Shakespeare) a sermon in stone, then La Sagrada Família is a sermon in broccoli. And none the less powerful for it.

On inspection, Gaudí's architecture isn't whimsical at all. His dedication to something even bigger than the ego of an architect sets him apart from others who have built odd and surprising buildings. Art Nouveau got its inspiration from nature. The Bauhaus got its inspiration from engineering. Critics have said Frank Gehry gets his inspiration from crumpled pieces of paper. Gaudí had inspiration already, and nature showed him God's engineering.

VINCE PASSARO

Scorsese on the Cross

FROM *Harper's Magazine*

> *I wanted to be a priest. However I soon realized that*
> *my real vocation, my real calling, was the movies. I don't*
> *really see a conflict between the church and the movies,*
> *the sacred and the profane. Obviously, there are major*
> *differences, but I can also see great similarities between*
> *a church and a movie house.*
> —MARTIN SCORSESE

ON THE WALL OF MY KINDERGARTEN CLASSROOM AT ST. ALOYSIUS School, among the many typical decorations, hung a gaudily colored print that I used to stare at with fascination. It featured Jesus kneeling in a stone chamber, wrists chained to the wall, head pricked with thorns, back bloody. Behind him stood a centurion: menacing, muscular (I mean really, *really* muscular), leather-clad, wielding an alluring (to a male child) cat-o'-nine-tails studded with shiny bits of metal—the better to tear open the skin of the scourged. I loved this picture, and wished ardently to own it, for reasons much clearer to me now than they were back then.

When I was a little older, I used to practice the Crucifixion at home in my room. I would stand in my underwear, bare back pressed to the cool plaster wall, with arms outstretched and one foot on top of the other. I was, to use an expression I didn't then possess, channeling the experience. It was quite a powerful feeling, and like the insane print, it was indisputably erotic. One of the many honed ironies of Catholic culture in America, then far more than now, was that a group so viciously opposed to any expression of eros poured such intense (if unacknowledged) erotic imagery into the heads of its children.

All of which is to say that for any mid-twentieth-century child with a dramatic sensibility and a seriously Catholic upbringing, no narrative can ever surpass the Passion, nor can any scene approach the Crucifixion for its depiction of agony and transcendence. The details of Jesus's final moments are especially haunting, none more so than the cry of abandonment recorded in Matthew and Mark. "And at the ninth hour, Jesus shouted in a loud voice, '*Eloi Eloi lama sabachthani?*' which is translated, 'My God, my God, why have you forsaken me?' " To a child, this line is frightening and, in its heroic isolation, exquisite. We were taught that the power of the divine, an unimaginable breadth of knowledge and potency, could reside in human suffering. For us, the merger of divine and human was mesmerizing, and beautiful, and extremely important—cosmically important.

So affirms Martin Scorsese in an exchange with the film critic Richard Schickel. The director, born in 1942 and raised in Little Italy with the Church and the movies as his lone sources of authenticity, is trying to account for the enormous controversy that greeted the release of *The Last Temptation of Christ*:

> *Scorsese:* . . . yes, you're talking about [divine] revelation
> and that's what we have to deal with. But we wanted

to talk about those other things—about Jesus, Judas, Mary, too . . . Paul Schrader [called it] "the dirty parts." Funny.

Schickel: What dirty parts?

Scorsese: Well, the concept that Jesus would have sexual feelings.

Schickel: Oh, that.

Scorsese: This was the big issue. That's what the critics claim it was.

Schickel: But this character is, for better or worse, half man and half God.

Scorsese: Oh, no, he's full man and full God . . .

Schickel: Whatever.

Scorsese: That's the beauty of it. Let's accept him as completely God and completely man, and therefore he's going to feel everything a man feels.

Schickel: Of course.

Schickel says *Whatever* and *Of course* because the distinction seems a trivial matter to him—as does, say, the complexity of the NFL pass interference rule to someone who doesn't care about football. But to an educated Catholic, his description of Christ as "half man and half God" mentally cues the red light and buzzer that follow the wrong answer on a quiz show. And note Scorsese's follow-up: "That's the beauty of it." For a Catholic artist, beauty actually resides in the incomprehensibility of the thing, in its (to steal the architect Robert Venturi's phrase) complexity and contradiction.

In fact, once the pieties of the candle and the novena have been peeled away, much of Christian doctrine is surprisingly hospitable to paradox. To accept a single being as "completely God and completely man" requires an ironic mind. Scorsese certainly has one, and this aspect of his art has kept him from being as popular as his studiously sincere and sentimental peers, including George Lucas, Steven Spielberg, and the latter-day Francis Ford Coppola.

As I read *Conversations with Scorsese*, in which Schickel and the director discuss each of his films in chronological order, the imagery of the Crucifixion kept coming to mind, both brutal and (to repeat the word) exquisite. And the more I watched many of these films again, some for the fifth or sixth time, the more I saw the pattern of Scorsese's religiosity played out, over and over, in dozens of intricate and spectacular forms.

Repeatedly Schickel insists that Scorsese's "great theme" is betrayal. Repeatedly Scorsese concurs, talking about the world of his youth and the kinds of men and women of Little Italy who formed his early understanding of what we call society. We see this world laid out clearly in *Mean Streets*, in which a small-time hood named Charlie (Harvey Keitel) is warned to abandon the two people closest to him: his friend Johnny Boy (Robert De Niro), and his lover, Teresa (Amy Robinson). In the end he is undone by his refusal to betray either of them. But what we detect emotionally from Charlie, and from Scorsese's use of the camera, is his perpetual isolation. Johnny Boy is far too flighty and indirect to be actual company: he is a responsibility, a burden, albeit a burden of love. And Teresa is, well, a girl—someone Charlie wants, but at the same time must keep at bay. By the time the movie ends, he is bloodied and alone.

A similar denouement awaits Travis Bickle in *Taxi Driver*, Jake LaMotta in *Raging Bull*, Rupert Pupkin in *The King of Comedy*, and Sam "Ace" Rothstein in *Casino*—with Robert De Niro playing each of these avatars of seething isolation. The same thing can be said of Henry Hill in *Goodfellas*, or Jesus in *The Last Temptation*.

And then there is Newland Archer in *The Age of Innocence*, an adaptation of Edith Wharton's novel of nineteenth-century New York, a decorous story that would seem to preclude the emotional rawness and working-class rage that marks most of Scorsese's work. The film ends with Archer, played by Daniel Day-Lewis, alone on a park bench in Paris. His great love, long separated from him, is unseen in an apartment above. Watching him, you know that he is encased in a social chrysalis of solitude, and cannot possibly climb those stairs. He departs, alone.

Jump ahead to Scorsese's later films and you see that the isolation grows more harrowing. In *The Aviator*, the aging Howard Hughes (Leonardo DiCaprio) sequesters himself in a dark room, nails grown long, hair a snarled mess, surrounded by crumpled tissues and jars of his own urine. In *The Departed*, DiCaprio's character endures the sequestered existence of a long-term undercover cop—and eventually even this secret, tenuous connection to the civilized world is erased on a crooked detective's computer screen.

Shutter Island finds DiCaprio even more isolated, lost in a guilt-induced dreamscape (we are never more alone than in dreams). At the end of the film, his delusions exposed, he chooses a kind of neurological death over a lifetime of contending with his memories. Obliteration is not a punishment: obliteration will be a relief. You might even call it a redemption.

His conversations with Schickel suggest that Scorsese wishes to know himself, has endeavored mightily to know himself, but is so tied to the fate of his films that he cannot always distinguish between who he is and what they are. Still, without spelling it out, he conveys the nuanced and contradictory isolation that has defined him as a creature on our planet. Nobody is less alone than a child in an Italian working-class clan. Family is everything, family is all over you. Yet a stroke of imaginative intelligence or artistic ambition will separate you out like leprosy.

Moreover, for a child of Scorsese's background, the world was a rigidly defined place: you do this, you don't do this, if you open your mouth there's going to be trouble. He tells Schickel this story eight ways from Sunday. You don't become a filmmaker, or any other kind of artist—it's unimaginable. The first time Scorsese saw New York University, just a few blocks from where he grew up, was when he went to enroll.

Pondering Scorsese's work, I happened to hear a recent radio interview with Pat Cooper, the eighty-one-year-old Italian-American comedian (also the only Italian-American comedian I ever heard of), in which he described his family's hostility toward his career. They found his work not only incomprehensible but offensive—"being funny" was not a respectable way to make a living. Meanwhile, Cooper's description of the parameters of Italian-American working-class life could have come right out of *Mean Streets*: "You work Monday to Friday, Friday night you get paid, Saturday you go shopping, Sunday you eat macaroni, Monday you go back to your job. Shut up, raise your kids, and shut up."

Scorsese is an escapee of that world. Nowadays he is commonly regarded as America's greatest living director. In many people's eyes, that elevation took place at the Academy Awards in February 2007. During the weeks leading up to the show, there seemed little doubt that Scorsese, after five previous nominations and no wins, would be given the Best Director Oscar for *The Departed*. The picture—a remake of a Hong Kong police-corruption film called *Infernal Affairs*—is not Scorsese's best. It is not even his sixth best. Still, it is an excellent piece of cinema, deftly infused with his particular kind of psychological tension, and with the considerable narrative complexities always kept clear (which is more than one can say for the original).

When it came time for the award, out onto the stage walked Coppola, Lucas, and Spielberg, three directors of Scorsese's remarkable generation whose films account for ten of the American Film Institute's hundred greatest American movies. (Once Scorsese joined them, the number edged up to thirteen.) It was a moment no less lovely for being so blatantly orchestrated. And the tableau was meant to make a statement: these three had come to celebrate one who must finally, despite his more limited audience, be recognized.

As a gesture, this lacked neither authentic drama nor authentic honor. But it also misplaced Scorsese cinematically. If one could have raised the dead and positioned him amid his true directorial cohort, Scorsese's companions on the stage would have been John Cassavetes, John Ford, and Akira Kurosawa. All three possessed what the presenters at the Oscars never had (Lucas and Spielberg) or long ago relinquished (Coppola): a deep understanding of the tragic, an embrace of it as the highest form of narrative art.

This is the problem with Scorsese. He was supposed to give that stuff up, and he never has. Which brings us back to *The Age of Innocence*. When Scorsese was filming the final scene in Paris, even his director of photography asked him why Archer couldn't simply go upstairs and embrace his beloved. Scorsese replied: "He can't. He can't go up. That's what she loved about him." How to uphold the tragic vision when our culture has all but expunged it from our consciousness? In a Scorsese picture, no Archer will ever go up the stairs. Tragedy is inherently, necessarily, uncompromising. And it makes much of the audience, and those who market to it, squirm, with its painful and paradoxical insistence that our lives are ruled both by individual agency and the iron dictates of society, family, and fate.

Tragedy is so far off our cultural radar that Scorsese has rarely been accused of it. He has, of course, been accused of many other aesthetic crimes, most commonly that he celebrates violence. This is like saying that Dante celebrates sin, or that Proust celebrates snobbery. Scorsese is not celebrating our condition, he is recognizing it: recognizing what becomes of men separated from God, men who are lost. Don DeLillo, who grew up in a world much like Scorsese's, once described the lingering effects of Catholicism this way: "For a Catholic, nothing is too important to discuss or think about, because he's raised with the idea that he will die any minute now and that if he doesn't live his life in a certain way this death is simply an introduction to an eternity of pain. This removes a hesitation that a writer might otherwise feel when he's approaching important subjects, eternal subjects."

These are the stakes for Scorsese. These are his protagonists: men who will suffer and who cannot face down that eternity of pain. Aristotle, our primary architect of tragedy, understood (as did the authors of the Gospels) that to see and feel deeply the suffering of others helps us to endure our own. This is the redemption that art can offer, and this has been the key to Scorsese's survival. His understanding of these facts is what *actually* makes him America's greatest living director. Just no one can really say so. We've almost lost the words for it.

MELISSA RANGE

Incarnational Theology

FROM *New England Review*

after Jürgen Moltmann

"God suffers in us, where love suffers,"
writes the theologian of the cross,
the fate awaiting all God's lovers.

You are my beloved, says the Father
as his dove rips through clouds to bless
the Son with suffering. In us, where love suffers,

Christ's ache throbs closer than a brother's—
stabbing my breasts, my thighs, his loneliness,
the fate awaiting all God's lovers.

God takes on flesh and thinks he'll smother.
Reeling, obsessed, his heart a wilderness,
God's a mess, suffering in me as I suffer

over a torn leaf, a tore-up man, the others
I've tried to love, shorn to the bone and luckless
as the Son. What fate's awaiting all the lovers

who dwell in me as migraines, as a stutter
in the veins, whose loss grows in me like grass?
God suffers them gladly. In us, love suffers:
it's the grace awaiting all God's lovers.

PATRICK HENRY REARDON

A Many-Storied Monastic

FROM *Touchstone*

IN THE LATE AFTERNOON OF DECEMBER 17, 1968, THOMAS MER-ton's body was laid to rest at his Trappist monastery, Gethsemani Abbey, in Kentucky. During the hour that immediately preceded the funeral Mass, the bier was placed at the top of the nave in the monastery church, where—in accordance with ancient monastic custom—two monks stood and recited the Psalms for the repose of Merton's soul.

I was one of those monks.

During the ensuing four decades and more, friends have repeatedly asked me to write down personal memories of that extraordinary man, whom I knew during the last thirteen years of his life. Although I cannot imagine adding anything new or significant to the vast material recorded in the endless stream of books and articles written about Merton since that time, I have at length determined to jot down a few recollections, whatever their worth.

This is not an introduction to Thomas Merton, of which many are already available, but a short collection of personal memories, arranged more-or-less as they come to me, along with a critical assessment or two.

I have begun them by placing myself, once again, at Merton's bier, just before the funeral, because the images of that hour are most vivid in my mind, and it truly was my last "contact" with him.

Ironies & Paradoxes

Like everyone else associated with Merton, I was stunned by several ironies, incongruities, contradictions, and points of paradox that attended his death. Some of these, I'm afraid, may have distracted my praying of the Psalms that day.

Most unusual was the large group of visitors who journeyed to the monastery for Merton's funeral. This truly was extraordinary. With few exceptions, we were quite unaccustomed to seeing many non-monastics at our funerals. During my years at the abbey, we buried between twenty and thirty of the brethren, I suppose, nearly all of them octogenarians, men who had long outlived their families and the friends from their earlier life. So, except for the postcard obituaries mailed to other houses of the Trappist order, the death of a monk was scarcely noticed outside his monastery. Dom James Fox, Gethsemani's abbot during most of my time, was fond of summing up their lives as "unknown, unheralded, and unsung."

Merton, however, was famous—perhaps the most widely read "spiritual writer" of his time and arguably the most celebrated monastic figure of the twentieth century. Consequently, all the wire services carried the news of his passing, and his obituary appeared in newspapers and journals around the world. (*Newsweek*—or was it *Time?*—ran a double obituary of Merton and Karl Barth, who died on the same day, December 10, 1968.) Consequently, quite a number of visitors were in attendance at the funeral.

Other points of irony were discernable in the circumstances surrounding Merton's death, coincidences that drew attention to various aspects of his personality and preferences. For instance, the manner of his death—by electrocution—put many of us in mind of Merton's well-attested "impracticality" and his relative incompetence in matters mechanical. Indeed, the man's mechanical unsophistication—he typed his scores of books with two fingers—proved to be, on occasion, nothing short of dangerous.

For instance, a gaping hole on the long north section of the monastery's enclosure wall—an opening roughly the width of a truck—testified to Merton's uncertainty respecting the proper function of a brake. Also, there was a harrowing story of novices nearly decapitated by long, two-handed saws that were laid across a jeep—blades forward—when Merton, following the driving method he knew best, floored the accelerator and released the clutch with all possible speed. The jeep violently lurched a few feet and stopped dead. Young monks crossed themselves and blessed a merciful Providence.

Given Merton's lack of sophistication with mechanical things, none of us was surprised to learn that faulty wiring on a fan had brought about his death. This accident could have befallen any of us, of course, but to this day I am not convinced Merton had a clear idea what electricity was or how it worked.

Ironically, even Merton's burial involved the use of electricity—a fact that would have driven him, I have no doubt, to utter distraction and bedevilment. He doubtless expected to be buried just like all the other monks: His body would be washed, clothed in the monastic cowl, and placed in an open bier—no casket—with handles for the pallbearers. There would be no embalming, and the funeral would take place the day following his death. After the funeral Mass, he would be carried in solemn procession out to the cemetery, the monks singing "When Israel went forth from Egypt."

The bier would be set down beside an open grave. At this

point, the monastery's Infirmarian would climb down a ladder into the grave, where he would await the lowering of the body on a sort of sling, held by four other monks standing above the four corners of the grave. Next, the Infirmarian would lay the body right onto the clay, place a napkin over the face, and climb back up out of the grave. Then, while some monks chanted more Psalms, others would fill in the grave. That was—and still is—the normal procedure for the burial of a Trappist monk.

Not Merton. Dying abroad, he was conveyed to the abbey in a steel casket, which was deposited finally on a mechanical contraption set over the grave. At the appropriate time, a local mortician flipped the electrical switch on this device, which began to buzz and hum, as Merton's remains were mechanically lowered into the Kentucky sod. This spectacle left several of the brethren shaking their heads or rolling their eyes, and the same thought was in everyone's mind: "Good heavens! He would hate this."

A light, misty rain began to fall. In the months to come, our dear friend Father Dan Walsh (well known from *The Seven Storey Mountain*) advanced the claim that our damp garments—in apparent emulation of Gideon's fleece—became dry as soon as we re-entered the church. Well, maybe Dan's did.

And then there was the paradox attending the return of Merton's body to America. He had been electrocuted exactly one week earlier, while attending an international monastic conference about thirty miles south of Bangkok, Thailand. I never learned how the process of the return was arranged, but eventually the body of this lifelong pacifist and conscientious objector was handed over to the United States Air Force. Thus, all that remained of Thomas Merton, ardent critic of the war in Vietnam, was brought home in a military transport plane, along with the bodies of American warriors who perished in that conflict.

A Religious Syncretist?

The incongruities surrounding Merton's death were of a piece with those that marked his life. Everyone who knew the man commented on the contradictions and paradoxes within his vocation as a monk, priest, and writer. Indeed, much of Merton's writing—starting with *The Seven Storey Mountain*—was taken up with explicit reflections on that very subject. Much of what the early Merton wrote was, "Gosh, should I be writing? I'm a monk, for heaven's sake."

The life and writings of Thomas Merton raise intriguing questions, and it showed great insight on his part, I believe, that he often compared himself to the prophet Jonah. (Indeed, the texts used in his funeral contained this theme.) Just as the biblical story of Jonah ends with a question—"Should I not?"—so Merton's vocation and ministry have always struck me, as they did Merton himself, as "questionable," in the sense that they truly provoked conscientious inquiry.

This will surprise none of his readers or friends, I think, those familiar with the astounding complexity of his life and thought. It is a simple fact that Merton does not *fit* comfortably into any usual category of analysis. For this reason, he has never been easy to interpret, so that even his friends, in my opinion, have occasionally missed the mark.

One of these, Edward Rice, Merton's first biographer, had been close to him since their college days. Yet, I believe his biography (*The Man in the Sycamore Tree: The Good Times and Hard Life of Thomas Merton*, 1972) misunderstood its subject, chiefly Merton's interest in the religions of the Far East. To this day, those influenced by Rice's interpretation tend to regard Merton more as a spiritual theorist than a Christian.

Thus, a couple of decades ago a well-known Orthodox writer, learning that I had been a novice under Merton's tutelage, expressed misgivings about him: "It seems to me," he confessed, "that Merton was a writer first, a monk second, and a Christian last."

I was happy to dispel that impression. From my earliest meeting with Merton (at 4 P.M. on December 28, 1955) I was moved by the sense of his deep conversion, *metanoia*, and the humility that exuded from his person. He said to me, "I have reached the point in my spiritual life at which I am certain that I know nothing about the spiritual life."

In addition, it is a documented fact that Merton, unto the day he died, cultivated standard and traditional disciplines of Christian piety: the observance of the Canonical Hours, the daily recitation of the rosary, the habit of regular Eucharistic adoration, the constant recitation of the Jesus Prayer, and so forth. These were not the practices of a Buddhist.

Not all the monks at Gethsemani were equally impressed with Merton, but, as far as I am aware, not one of them ever expressed the slightest doubt about the depth of his commitment to Christ and the Christian faith. While Merton certainly appreciated the Bhagavad Gita and the classical sutras, he was no Alan Watts.

Nor, in my opinion, was he another Bede Griffiths. Unlike the author of *The Golden String* and *River of Compassion*, Merton showed no interest in the integration of Oriental philosophy and Christian theology. Indeed, he was careful to avoid it. It appears to me that he was interested in Zen only in terms of its practical ascetical applications. In a note added to his *Zen and the Birds of Appetite*, he declared, "any attempt to handle Zen in theological language is bound to miss the point."

Merton's study of India and the East was integral to his abiding concern with man's spiritual experience: spirituality. He read the ancient Oriental sources for the same reason he studied Plotinus, William Blake, and certain Mesoamerican poets: He culti-vated a mammoth curiosity about the religious experience of the human soul.

A Good Abbot

Another of Merton's mistaken biographers was Monica Furlong (*Merton: A Biography*, 1980), who blamed the complexities and difficulties of her subject's life on the unwarranted intrusions and virtual tyranny exercised by his overbearing abbot, Dom James Fox. In my opinion, Furlong's assessment was inaccurate to the point of injustice. Years later Dom James remarked to me, "In order to make Merton a hero, Furlong made me a Nero."

It is true that Merton more than once taxed the sympathies and patience of his abbot. Many of his pursuits—Zen asceticism, peace activism, the Civil Rights movement, Christian ecumenical dialogue, French Existentialism, the history of Communism, and a thousand other things—lay far outside the concerns and inter-ests of his abbot. Not to put too fine a point on it, Dom James was . . . busy. In addition to pastoring the 200 or so monks at Gethsemani, he had oversight of five other monasteries and fur-ther obligations in the service of the Trappist order.

But then, Dom James also had a responsibility for Merton, who would have been, in my view, an awkward handful all by himself. Over the years, I have pastored some difficult and com-plex individuals, but *no one* comparable to Merton. I have no idea how Dom James managed it.

In their styles of piety, the two men could hardly have been less alike. While Merton was endlessly complex, the abbot was relatively simple—a man of fervent devotion and a fairly uncom-plicated approach to the spiritual life. He was fond of simple spiritual aphorisms, which he invoked so often they started to sound like slogans. At any rate, his piety was utterly straightforward and uncomplicated. In contrast to Merton, who seemed to keep about twelve balls in the air at all times, his abbot did no juggling act.

One says a great deal about Dom James by mentioning his favorite book: Karl Adam's *The Christ of Faith*, a work that he read repeatedly—probably hundreds of times. Thus, his religious mind was entirely filled with, and shaped by, classical Nicene-Chalcedonian Christology. In his scheduled teaching to the monks, Dom James strayed never an inch from that theological framework. Over the years, at least one-third of his instructions to us were explicitly based on a single line from St. Benedict's "Instruments of Good Works": *Amori Christi nihil praeponere*— "to prefer nothing to the love of Christ."

The abbot's favorite motto, which struck some folks as a slogan, caught the essence of his piety: "All for Jesus, through Mary, with a smile." It would be hard to get less complicated than that.

Most prominent in that piety was a fierce devotion to the sufferings of Christ, endured as the price of man's salvation. The inscription on his abbatial coat of arms summed up this emphasis: *Deus Crucifixus*—"God Crucified." This theme entirely filled his life and, to the end, transformed his soul. When the mind of Dom James was not obliged to be thinking something else, it was preoccupied with the scourging at the pillar and the crowning with thorns. He was forever extending his finger to know the place of the nails.

Now, take a man like that, and put him in charge of Thomas Merton, an individual of unbounded curiosity and very quick intelligence, the enthusiast of a thousand interests, the voracious reader on an endless range of complex subjects, and the unflagging correspondent with hundreds of readers, friends, and adoring fans. There was no way for Dom James to keep track of all that, and he was certainly not in a position to assess the merits of everything within the vast range of Merton's interests. Sometimes he simply had to be cautious.

Four Concerns

Four things about Merton were of specific concern to Dom James, I believe:

First, Merton did not hesitate to go behind the abbot's back to get what he wanted. Very vivid in my mind is the morning our Father Prior announced that Dom James had just left for an emergency trip to Rome. In due course we learned why Merton had secretly appealed to the Vatican for permission to leave the Trappist order and join another order more to his liking.

Evidently, whoever was minding shop at St. Peter's when Merton's request arrived failed to spot and measure its significance. Learning of it late, a panicky Dom James caught the next Pan-Am flight to go over and explain the facts of life to somebody or other who had an office beside the Tiber: Thomas Merton—he pointed out—was the most famous member of the Trappist order. If he were to leave Gethsemani, the order would suffer irreparable damage around the world.

I would love to have been present when Dom James returned to Gethsemani and had his next meeting with his sneaky monk.

This was not the only occasion, I'm told, on which Merton attempted to catch his abbot napping. It was the sort of thing that tended to keep Dom James on his toes—and perhaps awake at night!

Second, Merton had constant health problems, partly because he was trying to live so many different vocations all at once: monk, writer, lecturer, correspondent, and commentator on an increasing number of subjects. He was frequently on the edge—and sometimes over the edge—of physical exhaustion. It affected his diet;

during my entire time in the monastery, Merton was never able to observe the monastic fast or eat at the common table. Even though one of our monks was a very skilled physician, Merton was often in Louisville for further medical consultation, testing, and treatment.

Third, Merton's personal stability was far from secure. Habitually impetuous, he was sometimes imprudent. Two of his best biographers, Michel Mott and Jim Forest—along with volume 6 of the published *Journals*—recorded the disturbing symptoms of a recklessness in Merton that came to the attention of his friends in the mid-1960s. It is no exaggeration to suggest that his emotional immaturity came close to compromising Merton's vocation and would surely have ruined his reputation, if Dom James had not intervened with a sympathetic heart but a firm hand.

Merton, never shy about admitting his shortcomings, and recognizing his debt to the abbot, went to some lengths to preserve the record of both his own problem and the abbot's intervention. One recalls St. Benedict's comment that good monks *want* an abbot over them.

Fourth, Dom James had reservations about Merton's many ties with the world, especially his growing fondness for travel. In 1968, with the election of Dom Flavian Burns (Merton's own student) as the new abbot, Merton's opportunities for getting away from the monastery suddenly increased, and Dom James, the retired abbot, was profoundly distressed on the point.

I know this for a fact. Talking with him a month or so after Merton's death, I was surprised by the frankness with which Dom James spoke of it. I quote: "His death was a blessing. Under the new arrangement, he would be gone from the monastery all the time."

Fox's concern was not simply for the general maintenance of Gethsemani's monastic discipline, but for the specific well-being of Merton's soul. He was vividly aware of St. Benedict's counsel: "The abbot must know that any lack of profit which the Master of the family shall find in his sheep, will be laid to the shepherd's fault."

I write these reflections as someone much closer to Dom James than to Merton. I knew him as a loving abbot, who endured a great deal from young and often rebellious monks, and none—I confess with repentance—more than myself. Looking back, after so many years, I marvel how my dear Father Abbot endured so much immaturity and insubordination on my part. He was infinitely patient and invariably kind.

I left the monastery six months after Merton's death, but Dom James Fox and I remained steady friends until the end of his life. We corresponded for many years, until his failing health no longer permitted it. I loved to visit with him whenever I returned to Kentucky.

When, in his closing years, he lodged in the monastery's infirmary, I would sometimes arrive at the chapel very late, a bit before midnight, in order to serve as the altar boy at his regular midnight Mass. This simple "Low Mass," which the abbot's devotion prolonged to as much as two hours, was celebrated very slowly, deliberately, and with great attention. From time to time, he would stop praying the text, close his eyes, and slip into deep communion with God. I knelt, all the while, and served him, as I had done as a very young monk, thirty years earlier.

The Novice Master

Indeed, let me go back to those earlier days and say more about my relationship to Merton himself.

Growing up in Kentucky and southern Indiana, I began visiting Gethsemani Abbey around 1950, when I was twelve. By age sixteen, I had pretty much resolved to join the monastery, but the Novice Master at that time, taking account of my inexperience and complete lack of education, told me to wait.

Then, in December of 1955, a few weeks before my eighteenth birthday, I learned that this Novice Master had become the abbot of a monastery on the Genesee River in New York. This meant that Gethsemani must now have a new Novice Master, so I went back for a "second opinion."

Learning that Merton, two weeks earlier, had become the new Novice Master, I asked to speak with him. To my surprise and joy, he suggested that I come back and join the abbey sometime during the following couple of months. I did so, arriving on the Feast of St. Gregory the Great, March 12, 1956, the first outside postulant to be received into Merton's novitiate. Until my tonsure as a professed monk in 1958, I was under his immediate tutelage.

Jim Forest has often mentioned the loud laughter he encountered on his first meeting with Merton. My own first experiences with Merton were not like that at all. At the time I joined the novitiate, he was only forty years old, and *The Seven Storey Mountain* had been published only eight years earlier. This was definitely the more austere, the pre-Vatican II, Merton.

Before arriving at the abbey, I had read everything he published up to that point, including *The Ascent to Truth, No Man Is an Island, The Waters of Siloe, A Man in a Divided Sea*, and *The Tears of the Blind Lions*. I had read *Seeds of Contemplation* five times.

We novices enjoyed the strong spiritual diet of Merton's lectures—four each week—covering Holy Scripture, the Church Fathers, monastic history and piety, and liturgical theology. It was from Merton that I first became familiar with the writings of John Cassian, the only Latin writer preserved in the Eastern Orthodox collection, the *Philokalia*. Merton likewise introduced us to the works of Augustine, John Chrysostom, Gregory the Great, and Bernard of Clairvaux. It was Merton who handed me my first book by C. S. Lewis, *The Screwtape Letters*, remarking, "You need to read this." In short, my early debt to him is immense.

I am especially grateful for Merton's serious introduction to Holy Scripture. I had always loved the Bible, but for the first time I began to study it in a systematic way, with the aid of modern exegetical resources. Father Hilarion Schmock, one of the other novices and a priest twenty years my senior, helped out in this respect. Merton asked him to translate a French pamphlet series on the biblical books, entitled *Pas-à-pas avec la Bible*, for the use of the novices. These translations were duplicated (by me) on a Neanderthal device called a "dittograph," which printed in purple ink.

Devouring these translations, I began to read the Bible with understanding and great relish—a joy that has continued through the ensuing half-century and more. I shall never forget how the Book of Jeremiah, for example, opened up to me as a novice, when I learned to read it in its historical setting: Josiah and the Deuteronomic reform, the fall of Nineveh, the rise of Babylon, the battle of Megiddo, the destruction of Jerusalem, and so forth. It was during the Trappist novitiate that my reading of Holy Scripture began to be transformed. I owe that original impulse to Merton and several other monks whom he had trained.

Above all, Merton taught us to pray. Two particulars should be mentioned:

First, the Psalms: I had begun to pray the Psalms as a child, and in the monastery we recited—I counted them—284 Psalms each week. During the summer prior to joining the monastery, I had read Merton's newly published *Bread in the Wilderness*, which introduced me to the Christological praying of the Psalter. He gave the novices copious tutelage on this theme, though I had no idea at the time that the Psalter would become a dominant preoccupation for the rest of my life.

Second, repetitive prayer: Merton also introduced us to the practice of "the Jesus Prayer," the sustained repetition of the formula "Lord Jesus Christ, Son of the living God, have mercy on me, a sinner." (At the time, as I recall, he was reading articles on the Jesus Prayer in the Belgian journal *Irenikon*.) I adopted this form of prayer with a steady application, and it is still one of the most important components of my relationship to God. Some years ago, *Touchstone* published an article of mine on this subject ("The Prayer of the Publican," Fall 1996).

At the time I joined the novitiate, Merton's interests seemed to lie chiefly in the Fathers of the Church and the literature of Christian mysticism. This was still the case, I believe, when I was tonsured in late spring of 1958 and moved over to the "professed side" with the other monks. This was the year Merton published *Thoughts in Solitude*, a work in which there was no sign, as yet, that things would soon change in a very big way.

The Change

On October 9 of that year, Pope Pius XII died, and twenty days later the Sacred College elected Pope John XXIII. For those who did not actually live through it, I suspect it is impossible to appreciate the full force of the enormous upheaval we were about to experience. I, for one, was not even slightly prepared to deal with it.

On January 25, 1959, the new pope announced his intention of summoning a special worldwide synod of bishops. If there were doubts about the intent and purpose of the coming synod, they were dispelled by the pope's several comments about "opening the windows" to let some fresh air into the Roman Catholic Church.

The work of preparation, which was unbelievably extensive, included reassessments of the Church's many auxiliary institutions—including monasticism. By the time the Second Vatican Council was officially announced on Christmas of 1961, preparations for it had already progressed at a steady pace. Within the limits imposed by Trappist silence, the coming synod was "all the talk." At last, the bishops met on October 11, 1962; the synod came to an end on December 8, 1965.

Among those who answered the pope's summons to open the windows, I wonder if anyone was more responsive than Thomas Merton, a fresh-air enthusiast if ever there was one. Although I cannot speak of this matter firsthand (as I was no longer under his tutelage), a sequential examination of Merton's writings, especially his *Journals*, shows the development—during that period—of his expanding interest in certain subjects that were placed on the agenda of the coming council: social justice, world peace, and religious dialogue with non-Christians.

Merton's opportunities to write about these things increased dramatically in 1965, when he retired as Novice Master and moved to a modest home out in the woods north of the abbey. This house was always referred to as the "hermitage," but I would not push that designation too strictly. It was there that Merton met with scores of visitors, who came to consult him—alone and in groups—on every matter under the sun. They were as diverse as Jacques Maritain and Joan Baez. Merton was never more in contact with the problems and concerns of the world, one suspects, than during those three years he lived all *alone* in the woods.

To gain some sense of the wide shift of perspective brought about in Merton's mind during the 1960s, it suffices, I think, to compare two of his autobiographical works: *The Sign of Jonas*, which chronicled his life from 1946 to 1952, and *Conjectures of a Guilty Bystander* (1966), which chronicled the years right before and during Vatican II. The chief contrast between these two works, I submit, is found in the relative amount of space each volume devotes to matters and preoccupations *outside* the monastery.

In fact, once the bishops had settled themselves in Rome, they received a letter from Thomas Merton, who shared his own ideas about the opening of windows.

For his part, Merton certainly kept them open. A few weeks after he died, his very able literary secretary, Brother Patrick Hart, asked me to come to his office to inspect something special that had just arrived in the mail. Brother Patrick handed me some spiral notebooks, the pages of which were filled with Merton's distinctive but difficult script, along with some photographs he had pasted in.

These were Merton's last writings, sent to Brother Patrick from Thailand. I looked through the material and, on his request, translated a couple of Greek quotations that Merton had entered. In these pages, there was evidence of his vast reading during the last months of his life. I particularly recall a quotation or two from Hermann Hesse, an author I happened to be reading at the time.

In 1973 this rich trove, along with some letters and other pieces, finally appeared as *The Asian Journal of Thomas Merton*. It was the first project in the long and steady publication of his posthumous works, directed by the Thomas Merton Center in Louisville. This institution, which belongs to Bellarmine University (where I served on the faculty from 1969 to 1974), carries on the legacy, making the unique and valuable *Mertonia* available to visiting scholars.

Assessment

After leaving the Gethsemani novitiate in 1958, I had far less contact with Merton, though we both still belonged to the same monastery. Care of my soul and education was turned over to other monks, some of whom had been Merton's students in earlier days. These were teachers of marvelous competence, two of whom became authors of important works on liturgical and/or monastic theology: Dom John Eudes Bamberger and the late Father Chrysogonus Waddell. My debt to both these men, though it is beyond reckoning, is gladly attested.

As for Merton during those final ten years, various authors have traced the lines of his intellectual and literary development, perhaps none with greater clarity than the Baptist historian James Thomas Baker, author of *Thomas Merton, Social Critic* (1971).

Although Merton's interests *developed* extensively during the 1960s, his readers—and even friends—are far from agreed whether that development necessarily represented an improvement. Nor will I try to settle the matter here.

It is worth observing, nonetheless, that Merton interpreted that later process not as an evolution but as a *repudiation* of his earlier work. Even making allowance for hyperbole in his declarations on the matter, it is difficult to escape the impression that *The Seven Storey Mountain* genuinely embarrassed the later Merton.

Well, his books are all out there and available, so let everybody choose his favorite. For my part, I regard *The Seven Storey Mountain* as Merton's absolutely best book and the one most likely to be read a century from now.

As I reflect on those days of old, perhaps I may be permitted to mention a wishful reverie or two:

First, I admit a strong partiality favoring the Merton of the mid-1950s, *before* the preparations for Vatican II. At that earlier period, Merton seemed more engrossed in sacred theology. Since I love the study of theology above all things, I sort of wish Merton had done more of it.

Correspondingly, I have never been able to appreciate Merton's great interest in non-biblical religions. This is just a personal observation, however, not a criticism. *Non possumus omnia omnes*.

Second, I sort of wish Merton had avoided political activism. It is not that I was in material disagreement with the various individual stands that he adopted on political questions. I was distressed, rather, that Merton's attitude *in re politica* seemed to be determined entirely—I want to say, blindly—by unexamined liberal presumptions. I truly wonder if, even once in his life, Merton ever sat down and spoke seriously with a competent political or economic conservative. (Well, Maritain, yes, but I suspect the two of them avoided talking together about politics.) In political matters, Merton was very much the echo of the Ivy League elite.

Third, I rather wish Merton had spent more time (time subtracted from Oriental studies and those pesky political concerns!) to write literary criticism. Truth to tell, literature was his long suit. I think, for instance, of his critical notes on Camus' *The Plague* (which included his devastating critique of Teilhard de Chardin), his analysis of Flannery O'Connor, his assessments of (and correspondence with) Boris Pasternak, and the myriad comments he offered, here and there, on Ionesco, Peguy, Bernanos, Sartre, Rilke, Kafke, Hemingway, Mauriac, and many others. I wish we had more literary studies from Merton.

Final Blessing

Over the years, I have several times been introduced as a "disciple of Thomas Merton." I let it go a time or two, but I finally put my foot down: I am *not* a disciple of Thomas Merton. He was a teacher and friend in my youth; indeed, he was one of the most remarkable men it has been my privilege (and advantage) to know. But I am not a disciple or enthusiast of Merton.

Not since I left the Trappist novitiate in 1958 have I once quoted Merton as an authority on any subject whatever. This is not a criticism of him. It is a matter of my own approach and preference. I am simply incapable of looking at Merton as an authority on much of anything. (Nor, as far as I can tell, did Merton think of himself as any kind of authority.)

In particular, my soul has never felt comfortable with Merton's sustained emphasis on the cultivation of religious experience. He always seemed to me too preoccupied with that component of subjectivity which separates spirituality from *pietas*. I must confess that I have never, in my adult life, felt much interest in "spirituality." I have had this problem with Merton since as early as 1960, I think.

This confession is no criticism of Merton, of course. It says something only *about me*, and explains why I am less than sympathetic to Merton's approach to the human soul. I believe he was at his best when he was restricted by the rough, objective structures imposed by pre-Vatican II monasticism: the years of the *Mountain*.

On the other hand, it is perhaps the case that Merton left his mark on me deeper than I know.

I am certain of this much: My memories of him are warmly cherished—his exuberance and sharp wit, the agility of his imagination, his compassion, his capacious intellect, his love of living things, his profound humility and personal resilience, his enthusiasm for study and prayer, and the sarcasm he occasionally doled out to the deserving. Sometimes even his faults—his impetuosity and frequent displays of annoyance—were endearing. Or at least entertaining!

I was able to share some of these memories last year, when my gentle friend Jim Forest invited me to accompany him and a couple of other Merton enthusiasts to visit Gethsemani and spend the day. This was absolutely delightful. We lunched with Brother Patrick Hart, and Brother Paul Quenon (Merton's novice a couple of years junior to me) hosted the four of us at the "hermitage" for the afternoon. Of us four, Forest and I were the only ones who actually knew the living Merton, and the discussion profited from the fact that we knew him from—and approached him from—such different directions.

Anyway, I am grateful to Jim Forest for that invitation. It was a most memorable day, and I suspect that our wonderful time together may have been the impetus I needed to jot down, at last, these few recollections of a truly remarkable man it was my joy to know in olden times.

MARILYNNE ROBINSON

What We May Be

FROM *Harper's Magazine*

> Behold, I shew you a mystery; We shall not all
> sleep, but we shall all be changed, in a moment,
> In the twinkling of an eye, at the last trump:
> for the trumpet shall sound, and the dead shall be
> raised incorruptible, and we shall be changed.
>
> —I CORINTHIANS 15:51–52

THE WHOLE OF PAUL'S FIRST LETTER TO THE CORINTHIANS IS beautiful. But just here there is a rise in the language, a pent joy, a vision under profound restraint, that is like nothing else. "Lo! I tell you a mystery," as the Revised Standard Version has it, "We shall not all sleep, but we shall all be changed, in a moment, in the twinkling of an eye." Paul is telling his new converts that, at the end of things, we will be changed from human beings into human beings, from the first Adam to the second Adam—"Just as we have borne the image of the man of dust, we shall also bear the image of the man of heaven." Ophelia says, "Lord, we know what we are, but know not what we may be." It is the voice of life, disheartened with itself and yearning for more life, for the other self or selves we know most intimately in their elusiveness.

The phrase "in the twinkling of an eye" appears here first in the fourteenth-century translation of the Latin Vulgate made by John Wycliffe and others. Paul wrote in Greek "in the blink of an eye," and Jerome rendered this faithfully as *in ictu oculi*. The Wycliffites took a word from the unaccountably rich vocabulary the ancestors of the English language created to mark subtle differences in the appearance of light, enabling all their generations of descendants to distinguish a glitter, a glimmer, a shimmer. Or the translators simply adopted an idiom. This was the period of Chaucer and Langland, when a robust vernacular literature flourished, taking its pleasures from the vividness and ingenuity of common speech. In Chaucer one finds "hise eyen twynkled" and "a litel shymeryng of a light." So far as I can discover, every major English translation has followed Wycliffe in this detail, including the King James Version of 1611.

This very ingratiating, very human image seems to me to interpret the passage, or to leave a trace of the intention with which Wycliffe and others around him did their work. Wycliffe, an Oxford professor, was burned for his labors. He died a natural death but was exhumed in order to be burned, a fact that speaks tellingly of the potency of the barrier he had breached with his translation. At the time his Bible was first circulating, the great Peasants' Revolt, a failed rebellion against poverty and repression, had just ended, and this no doubt made the populism of the project particularly objectionable to the authorities. And in fact Wycliffe was associated with a movement called Lollardy. The Lollards were preachers, at first Oxford students, who went out under cover of night to read to the poor in the countryside from the English Bible. They were violently suppressed, yet their movement persisted into the sixteenth century, when it merged with the Reformation.

These days the Bible seems to be used largely to shore up

authority, or to legitimize political interests that claim a special fealty to Christianity. The Bible is much thumped and little pondered. So it may not be obvious why people living in the Middle Ages who enjoyed the rare privilege of literacy would have put themselves at terrible risk in order to carry Scripture into the hovels of the poor and defeated. "Gospel" is itself an old English word meaning glad tidings or good news. So perhaps enough of the first meaning still clung to it to give Wycliffe's translation of *evangelium* as "gospel" a special power.

"Beholde I shewe a mistery unto you." These are the words of William Tyndale, another Oxford scholar, who completed his version of the New Testament in 1526. But he was, he said, making a translation that a plowman would understand. Much of the celebrated beauty of the King James Bible is owed to Tyndale, and to his imagined readership, the plowman, whose language he returned to him in this extraordinary, very loving work. Tyndale was burned for his labors.

These are the origins of the Bible in English, the vehemently unauthorized precursors of the Authorized Version of 1611, or the King James Version, as we call it in America. Its greatness is owed in large part to the fact that it has preserved much that is best in the work of its martyrs, including a sense of the urgent generosity that lay behind their words. Imagine a tonsured youth taking a page or two of Scripture from his sleeve and kneeling to read, by some small, furtive light that, since it played on English faces, flickered or gleamed. "We shall all be chaunged, and that in a moment, and the twincklynge of an eye." He'd have been reading to old Adam the delver, the man of earth, the bearer of the primordial curse whose toil was grossly embittered by the impositions of his fellow men. And in the quiet of the peril they shared he'd have brought him the vision of himself as the new Adam, not burdened and coerced by the needs of his hungry body and by the entrapments of his degraded condition, but wholly conformed to himself as a living soul. We know what we are, but we know not what we may be. Anyone who speaks English understands what is meant by the twinkling of an eye, that genial look of inward pleasure that cannot be mistaken and cannot be feigned. It passes even between strangers like a shared secret, a sign of deep human recognition. Lo, I tell you a mystery.

ABDULLAH SAEED

The Islamic Case for Religious Liberty

FROM *First Things*

THE WORDS OF THE QUR'AN AND HADITH CONTAIN RICH resources for supporting the democratic order. If Muslims are to embrace modernity, including life in a pluralistic, democratic society, without abandoning their faith, they must take up the argument for religious liberty that is embedded in their history and that stands at the center of their most sacred texts.

Although the broad thrust of the Qur'an and hadith supports religious liberty, many parts of these texts can be, and traditionally have been, interpreted as denying it. One example is a qur'anic verse that deals with the question of the *jizyah*, a tax on non-Muslims: "Fight those who believe not in Allah nor the Last Day, nor hold that forbidden which hath been forbidden by Allah and His Messenger, nor acknowledge the religion of Truth, [even if they are] of the People of the Book, until they pay the Jizyah with willing submission, and feel themselves subdued" (Q 9:29). The Prophet reportedly sometimes demands the death penalty for apostasy, the most obvious example of this being the hadith "Whoever changes his religion, kill him" (Bukhari, *Sahih*, 9, 84, hadith 57).

These problematic texts are outweighed by the bulk of the texts and instruction provided by the two most important authorities in Islam, the Qur'an and the Prophet Muhammad's actual practice. Both are remarkably supportive of the idea of individual and personal religious freedom.

The bedrock of the Islamic case for religious liberty is the Qur'an's vision of the human person. The Qur'an's anthropology—which is shared by Christianity and Judaism—views every human being as a creation of God, blessed with intellect and free will. God created humans "in the best of molds" (Q 95:4) and in doing so honored humanity and conferred on it special favors (Q 17:70). The Qur'an emphasizes that human beings have inherent worth and dignity. Further, it holds that God gave humankind the intellect and ability to discern between right and wrong (Q 17:15 and 6:104).

The Qur'an emphasizes free choice. "The truth [has now come] from your Sustainer: Let, then, him who wills, believe in it, and let him who wills, reject it," it says (Q 18:29). And also: "Whoever chooses to follow the right path follows it but for his own good; and whoever goes astray goes but astray to his own hurt" (Q 17:15). Resoundingly, the Qur'an declares that "there shall be no coercion in matters of faith" (Q 2:256). Belief is an individual choice—or, rather, it is a choice involving the individual and God. Therefore forced conversions are simply unacceptable, and anyone who would use force rather than persuasion to promote religion must ignore the view of the person central to the Qur'an.

The capstone of the qur'anic case for religious liberty is the fact that not even the Prophet Muhammad could impose or force people to profess Islam. When people were unreceptive to the message of Islam, the Qur'an explicitly reminded him that he was never to resort to coercion: "Your task is only to exhort; you cannot compel them [to believe]" (Q 88:21).

Evidence from Islamic history suggests that this view was held not only by Prophet Muhammad but also by his political successors. In one recorded example, an elderly Christian woman came to see the caliph Umar and then refused his invitation to embrace Islam. He became anxious that she might have perceived his invitation as compulsion. "O my Lord," he said, expressing his remorse, "I have not intended to compel her, as I know that there must be no compulsion in religion. . . . [R]ighteousness has been explained and distinguished from misguidance."

Unfortunately, many Muslim-majority countries have failed to follow the Prophet's example. Muslims in these states face penalties for blasphemy, heresy, and, most famously, apostasy. Non-Muslims are barred from proselytizing and possessing or importing unsanctioned religious items, including Bibles. They face restrictions on the public practice of religion and strict limits on the building or renovation of places of worship. The government monitors their religious activities, raids private services, and sometimes harasses or imprisons non-Muslim believers simply for practicing their faith.

But the Qur'an says much to undercut such restrictions. On a practical level, it repeatedly emphasizes the role of the Prophet as teaching people about God rather than forcing them to convert to Islam. "The Apostle is not bound to do more than clearly deliver the message [entrusted to him]" (Q 24:54). Similarly, it urges readers to "pay heed, then, unto God and pay heed unto the Apostle; and if you turn away, [know that] Our Apostle's only duty is a clear delivery of this message" (Q 64:12).

In fact, the Qur'an appears to afford a high degree of freedom to non-Muslims under Muslim rule, particularly Jews and Christians (sometimes known as the "people of the book"). Its relatively tolerant position gave way to restrictions that emerged approximately one hundred years after the death of Muhammad. At the time of the Prophet, the Qur'an clearly distinguished between those non-Muslims who were hostile to the emerging Muslim community and were prepared to use violence against it and those non-Muslims who desired to live peaceably. In passages from the last two years of the prophet's time in Medina (631–32 C.E.), the Qur'an encouraged, and even commanded, Muslims to bring these hostile forces under the authority of the Muslim state. However, even when exhorting Muslims to fight their opponents, the Qur'an did not suggest that those engaged in hostilities should be forced to convert to Islam. Indeed, it drew a sharp line between enforcing recognition of state authority and forcing any change of religious belief.

So the Qur'an does not endorse use of the sword to force conversions to Islam. But does it command such means to stop conversion *from* Islam?

The answer, I believe, is no. The Qur'an itself does not prescribe any worldly penalty—let alone death—to those who leave Islam. There are two clear categories of apostasy in the Qur'an. The first concerns Muslims who profess Islam outwardly but who then attempt to destroy the Muslim community from within, using every opportunity to discredit the Prophet (Q 2:8–18). However, the Qur'an does not recommend the death penalty even for this group of religious hypocrites, or *munafiqun*.

The other category of apostasy concerns Muslims who reject Islam and then return to it, only to reject it again a second or even a third time, seesawing back and forth between Islam and their former religions (Q 4:137). In the case of these serial apostates, the Qur'an does not suggest the death penalty. It specifies only a severe punishment that they will suffer in the life after death—the same otherworldly punishment the Christian tradition reserved for apostates.

And in fact, in the first centuries of Islam after the Prophet's death, when the community was more threatened from outside forces, the laws prohibiting apostasy, blasphemy, and heresy were used often against political and theological opponents, whereas at other times Muslim critics of Islam were allowed to remain and function within the Muslim community despite their controversial views.

That is the qur'anic teaching. What do the hadith, the collected traditions and sayings of the Prophet, say about religious liberty? Some appear to indicate that any Muslim who changes his or her religion should be killed. However, the hadith themselves offer no evidence to suggest that Prophet Muhammad himself ever imposed the death penalty for the mere act of conversion from Islam. For example, a hadith in Bukhari's collection (one of the most important collections of hadith for Sunni Muslims) tells of a man who came to Medina and converted to Islam. Shortly after his arrival, however, he informed Prophet Muhammad that he wanted to return to his former religion. Far from punishing him with death, the Prophet let him go free, without imposing any penalty at all (Bukhari, *Sahih*, 9, 92, hadith 424). A contradiction, therefore, exists between certain sayings attributed to the Prophet and his actual conduct.

Of course, there are instances when the Prophet did impose the death penalty. What are we to make of them? In these cases, the accused had joined an enemy camp, or taken up arms against the Muslim community, or done something else that made their act more than a simple conversion. One version of an important hadith says: "A man who leaves Islam and engages in fighting against God and His Prophet shall be executed, crucified, or exiled" (Abu Duwad, *Sunan*, 33, hadith 4339). The crime being singled out for punishment is not the simple changing of one's faith but rather the definite choice to engage in war against the Muslim community.

Another hadith, attributed to the Prophet, affirms the idea that it is not simply a change of religion that warrants the death penalty for apostasy: "The blood of a Muslim who professes that there is no God but Allah and I am His Messenger is sacrosanct except in three cases: in the case of a married adulterer, one who has killed a human being, and one who has abandoned his religion, while splitting himself off from the community" (Muslim, *Sahih*, 16, hadith, 4152). The reference here to "splitting himself off from the community" is interpreted to mean one who actively boycotts and challenges the community and its legitimate leadership.

The various hadith that appear to command Muslims to kill apostates from Islam must, therefore, be understood in their proper political context. Most Muslim scholars today rely on the legal reasoning of the classical jurists without considering whether their reasoning should be considered authoritative or how changed political and legal conditions should shape our reception of that tradition's authoritative elements. In the view of Muhammad Mutawalli al-Sha'rawi, for example, a preacher from Egypt, the liberty of a Muslim is restricted in that a Muslim may not leave Islam once he becomes a Muslim. He argues that although a person is free to believe or not to believe in Islam, once he has embraced the Islamic faith he is subject to all of its requirements, including the contemporary stand on apostasy and its punishment.

At the time of Prophet Muhammad there was no "state" as such. A tribal system was in place in much of Arabia in the sixth and early seventh centuries. With the rise of Islam and its consolidation in Medina during the last decade of the Prophet's life (622–32 C.E.), converts to Islam from various tribes joined a community that was political as well as religious. Given the ongoing hostility between the Muslims and their opponents, conversion from Islam generally meant that a person left the Muslim community and joined its opponents. Apostasy was the equivalent of treason.

If the Qur'an does not speak against religious liberty, and if the evidence from relevant hadith is weak, how can we account for the restrictions on religious liberty in Muslim-majority states? Most of these restrictions can be traced back to classical Islamic law. The classical legal texts from each of the surviving schools of Islamic law provide a range of restrictions on the religious liberty of both non-Muslims and Muslims. These are not inevitable developments of Islam's two most authoritative sources, the Qur'an and the Prophet's actual practice, but rather a contestable departure from them.

About one hundred years after the death of the Prophet, Muslim theologians and jurists during the Umayyad dynasty began to define *Muslim* and *community*. Discussions of relations between Muslims and non-Muslims and of Islam's superiority over other religions were intertwined with theological debates over matters such as free will, predestination, and the nature of God. These debates produced a wide range of positions and schools of thought. It was within this context of religious pluralism and conflict that Muslims had to deal with the problem of religious liberty.

Over time, limits on religious liberty for non-Muslims were added. These included restrictions on the building of places of worship, public readings of Scripture, and the ability of non-

Muslims to engage publicly in certain activities that Muslims considered forbidden (such as drinking alcohol) if these non-Muslims were living in Muslim communities. It is far from clear how consistently or stringently the restrictions were applied in practice. Like apostasy law, they may have been used only at particular times of uncertainty, difficulty, or tensions with an external enemy.

Although these restrictions have come to form an influential part of classical Islamic law, non-Muslims under Muslim rule generally have been granted the prerogative to manage their own affairs (including religious affairs) from the time of the Prophet Muhammad onward. This practice was adhered to in various Muslim empires (from the Umayyad through to the Abbasid and the Ottoman). One example is the "millet system" established by the Ottoman Empire. One of the major challenges for the Ottomans was finding ways to govern the broad array of people, religions, cultures, and languages contained within their empire. Under the millet system, the Ottomans gave people of various religious traditions the right to practice their own religion and preserved their places of worship, provided they recognized the Ottoman state and the superiority of Islam.

With these arrangements in place, Ottoman society remained generally free of large-scale religious conflict for centuries. Even the Jews fleeing persecution in Spain found that they were welcome in Ottoman lands. This tolerance did not necessarily result in full equality or equal citizenship (which are, in any case, relatively modern concepts even in the West), but non-Muslims nonetheless rose to prominence in many Muslim states.

Today there is some movement toward Muslim acceptance of religious liberty. In global legal terms, religious liberty receives its primary definition from Article 18 of the Universal Declaration of Human Rights, which has been incorporated into other international instruments such as the International Covenant on Civil and Political Rights (ICCPR) and the UN Declaration on the Elimination of All Forms of Intolerance and Discrimination Based on Religion or Belief. Many Muslim-majority states have even signed and ratified the ICCPR, which contains the wording of Article 18 of the Universal Declaration, with some minor changes. The article reads: "Everyone has the right to freedom of thought, conscience and religion; this right includes freedom to change his religion or belief, and freedom, either alone or in community with others and in public or private, to manifest his religion or belief in teaching, practice, worship and observance."

Though they may continue to flout these ideals, the many Muslim-majority countries that have accepted this statement have, in some minimal legal sense, already committed themselves to the ideal of religious liberty.

Sadly, the implementation of this standard continues to be painfully slow because of certain trends within Islam. At a time when a number of ultraconservative voices appear to be dominating the discourse in many parts of the Muslim world, Muslim scholars who advocate for religious liberty are fiercely opposed. They are often labeled as stooges of the West or accused of being apostates or heretics. Many such scholars in Muslim nations are imprisoned for their views or have their publications banned. My book *Freedom of Religion and Apostasy in Islam* was banned in the Maldives in 2008 after a targeted campaign against my coauthor (and brother) Hassan Saeed by certain politicians and an ultraconservative group.

Despite current challenges, the degree of freedom available to many Muslims, particularly those who are based in intellectually free societies (many of which are in the West), can be used to challenge those who threaten religious liberty. Muslims, who now make up roughly 20 percent of the world's population, have a political and religious duty to take into account the important values and norms that have extensive grounding in Islam's most sacred texts and its own tradition. In doing so, Muslim thinkers will be returning to their most important sources of authority, the Qur'an and the Prophet, in support of tolerance and religious liberty.

NICHOLAS SAMARAS

Spiritual Bouquet

FROM *The Antioch Review*

This card is to communicate that I have
performed a number of devotional acts
on your behalf, as an expression of sympathy.
For your soul, I visited the Village bar
where we were young together, and drank
a Black Russian, on the stool next to your absence.
Though I am not Roman Catholic, I prayed
in the eastern wind for you. I visited
your Danube river, once blue but now
muddy with modern progress. I ate dinner
at an Indian restaurant across the street
from the Camp in Dachau, intently watching
the closed windows as I chewed slowly.
I visited the poet Georg Trakl's childhood home.
All of this to chase you and bring you back.
I understand this card is in your family's tradition
that you might not have shared. Yet I crossed
over the border of the old Iron Curtain

into the forest of your village. I prayed
on the darkest green wind, the glen mist
rising. A number of devotional acts.
For your soul. For my need.
This card. To communicate.

ALGIS VALIUNAS

The Sanest Man Ever

FROM *Commentary*

THE MODERN ESSAY BEGAN WITH MICHEL DE MONTAIGNE (1533–1592), a member of the minor French nobility, a Bordeaux vintner, a political official pretty much in spite of himself, who retired from public life at the age of 37 to read, think, and set down his thoughts in some of the best prose ever. He remains the acknowledged master of the form. It is a form that accommodates all sorts of approaches from all sorts of masters: the consummate shrewdness cloaked in blunt efficiency of Francis Bacon, the sonorous cogitation in solemn periods of Samuel Johnson, the rough-hewn majesty of Henry David Thoreau, the languorous but eviscerating drollery of Lytton Strachey, the antic bomb-throwing of Karl Kraus, the magniloquent cerebral torments of Albert Camus. The approach that Montaigne favored is very much in fashion today among practitioners of the so-called familiar essay, who tend to be far less adept than their great forebear: the ramble through the brambles in which one collects every burr that happens to stick to one's person and then picks them off in no particular order.

Montaigne called his book *Essais*; the French *essayer* means to attempt, to try out, and the rather archaic English *to essay* is cognate. Montaigne was not trying to fix his thoughts in stone, to get things perfectly right once and for all; the *Essays* is the living record of thoughts on the move—strolling, ambling, stalking, galloping, pausing for reflection, doubling back to reconsider. Montaigne is not known for beginning with a particular end in mind. Detours grow divagations; oxbows sprout sinuosities. You could wind up anywhere from here.

There are 107 essays, ranging in length from mere squibs to a disquisition on religious faith and the inadequacy of reason that amounts to a book on its own. A selection of essay titles suggests the amplitude of his interests, though the writing itself often carries him far from the stated intention: "Of sadness," "Of liars." "That to philosophize is to learn to die," "Of the education of children," "Of friendship," "Of cannibals," "Of the inequality that is between us," "Of prayers," "Of drunkenness," "Of glory," "Of the greatness of Rome," "Cowardice, mother of cruelty," "Of three good women," "Of repentance," "Of vanity," "Of cripples," "Of physiognomy." The essays appeared in three volumes and were written over the course of 20 years, from 1572 to 1592; Montaigne was an unrelenting reviser, and modern editions feature superscripts A, B, and C to designate textual variants. The French prose is direct, unadorned, for Montaigne loathed literary frippery; still, it is rather difficult for a less-than-expert American reader, largely because of the antique spelling. Notable English translations include those of John Florio (1603), Charles Cotton (1686), and the excellent recent versions of M. A. Screech and Donald Frame. (It is Frame's translation that I will use throughout.)

Montaigne's preeminent interest was in human beings. Inhuman nature did not much concern him, though he wondered whether he was playing with his cat or his cat was playing with him. What interested him most about people was their variety and inexplicability. As he wrote in the first essay in the book, "By diverse means we arrive at the same end," "Truly man is a marvelously vain, diverse, and undulating object. It is hard to found any constant and uniform judgment on him." Accordingly, Montaigne considered his human object, including most especially himself, from every angle. Here he followed Socrates, there the Stoics, somewhere else Pyrrhonian Skeptics, who doubt everything, including their doubt, and their doubt of their doubt. Then again he dismissed all philosophy in favor of unreflecting Roman Catholic orthodoxy, yet he had little to say about Jesus Christ, and one might even gather that he supposed death to end the whole show, or at least that he entertained this un-Christian notion not at all frivolously. Montaigne despised scholarly showboats and pedantic drudges, but he was an exceedingly bookish man who professed to value learning in the service of moral improvement. The sheer love of knowing, however, seemed his real animating passion. Montaigne's often-stated vocation was to know himself, and to know all the sorts of men there were was essential to his calling, for the world's variety provided the best measure of his own nature.

About his own nature he didn't miss a trick. His sexual frankness makes him sound like a 21st-century man or like Geoffrey Chaucer. He prescribed the appropriate heft and delicacy of the male and female private parts, respectively; described his hoodoo cure for a friend's impotence; noted that he took care not to excite his wife unduly in bed, strictly for her own good; and observed that sometimes his other women went at it half-speed, "with only one buttock." But his worldliness was not merely earthy; it encompassed political nobility as well. Despite Montaigne's reputation as the seminal master of the personal essay, he writes often of the most eminent public men and historical matters of the highest moment. Yet in a sense, even these essays are personal: he was intimate with the superb Greek and Roman men of action—Alexander, Epaminondas, Alcibiades, Julius Caesar, Cato the Younger—who were the regular companions of his thought.

To think seriously is to question relentlessly, and at the center of Montaigne's thought is the question *"Que sçay-je?"* What do I know? It is the silent outcry of a suffering soul alone in the night in need of some consoling certainty; the shrug of a stand-up comedian, in the spirit of the everlasting question "What, me worry?"; the preamble to an inventory of his mental contents, the books he has read, the women he has slept with, the deepest friendship he has enjoyed, the jokes he loves to tell and retell, the times he has nearly died; the cool admission of a thinking man that, when he gets down to it, he knows that he knows nothing.

Alexis de Tocqueville famously eulogized Blaise Pascal, the 17th-century mathematical genius, desperate God-seeker, and fierce critic of Montaigne, for sacrificing his life to intellectual passion: the very intensity with which he thought wore him out and killed him off at 39. Pascal didn't want to question but to know, that his soul was eternal, that he was bound for salvation, that his terror at the silence of the night sky was groundless. Such spiritual importunity did not suit Montaigne; it was intemperate, he thought. For Montaigne, thinking was anything but a suicidal ordeal. Nature will send ordeals enough your way; it is a serious mistake to turn one of the most agreeable human activities into a do-it-yourself auto-da-fé. The crucial questions for Montaigne were not the Pascalian obsessions of asking why God put me here and where he will send me when I die, but rather, How do I best spend the time I have been given and which men and women do I really love or admire? It was the life of this world that engaged his passions.

And yet there appears to have been a fundamental—even a fundamentalist—religious belief underlying this contented worldliness. In "Apology for Raymond Sebond," the essay that takes up 139 pages of an 857-page volume and endeavors to demonstrate that human reason cannot fathom divine mystery, Montaigne finds more wisdom in simple piety than in the arrogant self-inflation of classical philosophy. He rips Democritus for proclaiming his capacity "to speak of all things," scorns Aristotle for prating of the best men as "mortal gods," lambastes Seneca and Cicero for saying God may have given them life but it is their own merit that made their lives good. And Montaigne settles with a peremptory slap the immemorial rumble between philosophy and poetry. They are both pure invention, contrived to accommodate puny human understanding. There is no form of nonsense that somebody or other has not turned into philosophy; Plato's heaven-as-an-orchard, for instance, is sheer malarkey. Plato's defenders might say he invented a puerile heaven for those incapable of philosophy, but Montaigne does not broach that possibility.

Philosophy is not alone in going wrong, however. Simple piety also has its charlatans who exploit men's wish for a heaven that will deliver what they most want from earthly life. As with Plato, "when Muhammad promises his followers a paradise tapestried, adorned with gold and precious stones, peopled with wenches of surpassing beauty, with rare wines and foods, I can easily see that they are mockers stooping to our folly to honey us and attract us by these ideas and hopes appropriate to our mortal appetites."

For his own part, Montaigne cleaves to a faith that nonbelievers may well find as preposterous as the Muhammadan jackpot of houris. The elaborate doctrine of the Roman Catholic Church, which must be accepted whole, provided him the one secure fixture in a world of intellectual flux that amounts to disorder or madness: ". . . when [reason] strays however little from the beaten path and deviates or wanders from the way traced and trodden by the Church, immediately it is lost, it grows embarrassed and entangled, whirling round and floating in that vast, troubled, and undulating sea of human opinions, unbridled and aimless." He stands by the faith into which he was born, largely because he was born into it, and because confusion lurks without: "And since I am not capable of choosing, I accept other people's choice and stay in the position where God put me." The argument, however, soon takes another turn: to adhere to the religion of one's country simply because it is one's country, as Socrates advised, represents gross spiritual failure. There exists a divine law that must be one's only guide, and that law has been revealed. But Nature has complicated matters for the truth of revelation. If Nature had clearly laid down a law for all men to follow, Montaigne avers, then all men would be following it. "Let them show me just one law of that sort—I'd like to see it." Instead, Nature has broadcast human variety and sown consternation. Because Nature does not comply with the revealed truth, conflict over the eternal questions is inevitable. In the absence of a universal natural law, "the eternal foundation of His holy word" and Holy Mother Church are what believers have to believe in. It is really by default that Montaigne convinces himself of this.

Montaigne does not take up fire and sword in the name of his faith, as many of his countrymen did during his lifetime. He clearly deplores religious murderousness, yet he is not exactly an ideal spokesman for universal tolerance and brotherhood. In the essay "Of husbanding your will," he writes about the "phantasms and dreams" that moved the men of his time to follow malignant spiritual and secular leaders into an earthly hell, and he compares these delusions to "the monkey tricks" of Apollonius, who claimed to understand animal language, and to Muhammad. Condemning your co-religionists for mad sectarian violence does not mean believing your faith any less true; nor does it necessarily mean believing another faith to be even respectable, much less as worthy of devotion as your own. Montaigne's religious sentiments are not the sort that pleases current liberal opinion; they are better left out of the picture or smudged discreetly.

Sarah Bakewell's recent biography, *How to Live, or A Life of Montaigne in One Question and Twenty Attempts at an Answer* (Other Press, 389 pages), is as good a book about Montaigne as one can hope for from an author pleasing to current liberal opinion. The 20 chapter headings suggest answers from Montaigne's recorded experience to the question in her book's title, which is really of a piece with, What do I know? How do I live? Don't worry about death. Pay attention. Survive love and loss. Be convivial. Live temperately. Guard your humanity. See the world. Philosophize only by accident. Be ordinary and imperfect. Let life be its own answer.

This list sounds like a compendium of the most banal and wearisome 21st-century liberal nostrums, and it is sadly true that what Bakewell most admires about Montaigne is his common ground with modern progressive thinking. Leonard Woolf's hailing Montaigne as the discoverer of how cruel human cruelty is, Virginia Woolf's loving him for understanding that life's only purpose is life itself: these are Bakewell's touchstones of Montaigne's excellence. As she writes: "The twenty-first century has everything to gain from a Montaignean sense of life, and, in its most troubled moments so far, it has been sorely in need of a Montaignean politics. It could use his moderation, his love of sociability and courtesy, his suspension of judgment, and his subtle understanding of the psychological mechanisms involved in confrontation and conflict. It needs his conviction that no vision of heaven, no imagined Apocalypse, and no perfectionist fantasy can ever outweigh the tiniest of selves in the real world."

The author is plainly admiring her own even-handedness here. Every religious believer who holds his faith to be singularly true, every patriot who is willing to fight for his country's freedom, or even for other countries' freedom, stands guilty before her, and presumably before Montaigne. It would supposedly detract from the spirit of Montaigne to place the blame for current political and religious monstrosity squarely where it belongs.

One regrets that Bakewell plays this angle with Montaigne. In spite of her determination to use him as a club with which to beat contemporary partisans, she has written a book elegant in style and fascinating in many respects, especially in its account of Montaigne's reputation in previous centuries. And it is not untrue that Montaigne did anticipate modern liberalism in certain ways. But he was more complicated and more interesting than Bakewell will allow. He bites sometimes, while she would prefer he gum you into peaceable submission.

Bakewell acknowledges Montaigne's fideism—his subscription to Catholicism on unreasoning faith—but she suggests that he was not really serious about it. She prefers to emphasize his distaste for the civil wars of religion, whose abominations she details with grisly vividness. She notes that Montaigne could be the descendant, on his mother's side, of Jewish refugees from Spain who were compelled to convert to Christianity; but there is no proof of his having had Jewish blood, Bakewell goes on, and no indication that he might have thought he had. It is hard to say whether this speculative throwaway is a biographer's due diligence or another gesture in the direction of Montaigne's incomparably full humanity, as though it would be richer if he had not been an ordinary French Catholic with somewhat exceptionable Catholic beliefs. And as for Montaigne's opinion of Muhammad, she knows better than to even mention that.

Like most liberals, and especially the liberal intellectual women who model themselves after Virginia Woolf, Bakewell far prefers the gentle ardors of private life to the dangerous inflammations of public life. Accordingly, she makes Montaigne out to be of a similar temper, and thus misrepresents his nature so that he would scarcely recognize himself. She mentions Alexander the

Great three times, and twice it is to register his brutality or that of his soldiers. But while Montaigne did indeed record these barbaric actions, they are hardly the whole story. In "By diverse means we arrive at the same end," Montaigne prefaces his account of Alexander's savage rage against a foe that fought on too long by commending the supreme conqueror as "the bravest of men and one very gracious to the vanquished." Admittedly, Bakewell could have also mentioned that essay's final paragraph, which relates Alexander's merciless slaughter of 6,000 Theban soldiers and the enslavement of 30,000 civilians. But even if she had, that would not have overridden Montaigne's esteem for Alexander. In "Of the most outstanding men," Alexander stands beside Homer and Epaminondas as the very best of the best. Alexander's subjugation of "all the habitable earth" was "the utmost achievement of human nature." As for certain instances of extravagant cruelty on his part, they are rationalized as unavoidable in so momentous an enterprise: "But it is impossible to conduct such great movements according to the rules of justice; such men require to be judged in gross, by the master purpose of their actions."

Still, one must confess that it is not Alexander but the Theban general and statesman Epaminondas who is the finest man in Montaigne's eyes. "In this man innocence is a key quality, sovereign, constant, uniform, incorruptible. In comparison, it appears in Alexander as subordinate, uncertain, streaky, soft, and accidental." The "exceeding goodness" even of the man remarkable at war singles him out for unique reverence.

But then there is "Of evil means employed to a good end," in which Montaigne extols the civic benefits of slaughter as a spectator sport. The sight of gladiatorial combat endowed the Roman people with souls of warlike steel: "It was in truth an admirable example, and very fruitful for the education of the people, to see every day before their eyes a hundred, two hundred, even a thousand pairs of men, armed against one another, hack each other to pieces with such extreme firmness of courage that they were observed never to let slip a word of weakness or commiseration, never to turn their back or make even a cowardly movement to avoid their adversary's blow, but rather to extend their neck to his sword and offer themselves to the blow." To see how far Montaigne goes in his admiration for martial nerve and ambition is disconcerting, to say the least, and not only for progressive ladies of exquisite sensibility. Pagan valor gets a lot more play in the *Essays* than does Christian virtue. Plutarch is Montaigne's gospel. Montaigne's admiration for the great political men of classical antiquity is consuming.

It would be wrong, however, to think that Montaigne scants the everyday or ignores his inner life. His concluding essay, "Of experience," offers his most detailed portrait of his idiosyncrasies. "And I cannot, without an effort, sleep by day, or eat between meals, or breakfast, or go to bed without a long interval, of about three full hours, after supper, or make a child except before going to sleep, or make one standing up, or endure my sweat, or quench my thirst with pure water or pure wine, or remain bareheaded for long, or have my hair cut after dinner; and I would feel as uncomfortable without my gloves as without my shirt, or without washing when I leave the table or get up in the morning, or without canopy or curtains for my bed, as I would be without really necessary things." He wants the reader to know of his fondness for oysters and melons, his wandering attention during sermons, the quickness of his step, the regularity of his bowel movements, his dislike of smoke and dust, the greed at table that makes him bite his tongue or even his fingers, the terrible pain of his kidney stones, the fortitude with which he endures the pain, the equanimity with which he faces death. "But you do not die of being sick, you die of being alive. Death kills you well enough without the help of illness." So *à la vie comme à la vie*: "When I dance, I dance; when I sleep, I sleep; and when I walk alone in a beautiful orchard, if my thoughts have been dwelling on extraneous incidents for some part of the time, for some other part I bring them back to my walk, to the orchard, to the sweetness of this solitude, and to me." There is no need for Plato's heaven; this world will do just fine. Passages such as these make Montaigne seem the sanest man ever, the paragon of simple good sense.

Yet sanity can be overrated; simple good sense, too, has its limitations and even its dogmatisms. There ought to be a place among the best men for celestial navigators such as Pascal, maybe even Swedenborg and Blake, or for that matter certainly Moses and Jesus. How to live? What do I know? There is a species of wisdom in spending one's life asking these questions and not expecting to get firm answers. Yet a serious man must also be able to say, *This* I know, *This* is how I live; and speculations about or intimations of a world beyond this one could have something to do with it. There may be a profound connection between Montaigne's professed religious belief and his willingness to entertain all manner of thoughts and feelings, to test their meaning specifically for him. Montaigne's anchor in Catholic orthodoxy permitted his mind to rove wherever it would yet never become unloosed from the confidence of faith. Perhaps he never troubled himself much about heaven as Pascal did because for him that was solid ground. It was this earthly world that shone for him like a gem of innumerable facets, and that he turned this way and that, catching the light from every direction, recording every glint and flash, seeing it all in a fashion uniquely his own, with a genius no essayist since has been able to equal.

GEORGE WEIGEL

All War, All the Time

FROM *First Things*

MARTYRDOM HAS BEEN AN INTEGRAL PART OF CHRISTIAN LIFE
since the Acts of the Apostles. Yet to many Christian minds, "mar-
tyrdom" is imaginatively confined to first-century Christianity—
a matter of Richard Burton and Jean Simmons defying Jay
Robinson's Caligula while Michael Rennie (St. Peter) looks on
paternally and a chorus of "Hallelujahs" brings *The Robe* to a
glorious Hollywood conclusion. This, however, is a serious mis-
conception of the history and geography of martyrdom. Modern
totalitarianism caused an effusion of blood *in odium fidei* that was
orders of magnitude greater than anything experienced before.
The Commission for New Martyrs of the Great Jubilee of 2000
concluded that there were likely twice as many martyrs in the
twentieth century than in the previous nineteen centuries of
Christian history combined.

The great majority of these twentieth-century martyrs gave their
lives for Christ at the hands of communism. Thanks to the new
political situation behind the old Iron Curtain it is now possible
to describe this almost-forgotten communist war against Christi-
anity in detail and to unlock some of its once closely held secrets.
For this was an undercover war as well as a matter of mass murder:

It involved spies and spymasters, moles and agents of influence, propaganda, disinformation, and other "active measures," just as it did slave labor camps and the bullet in the nape of the neck.

Over the past decade, research has begun in the archives of communist-era governments and secret police organizations in Berlin, Warsaw, Budapest, Prague, and even briefly in Moscow. My work on the biography of Pope John Paul II put me in contact with scholars mining this lode of information, several of whom shared materials and insight with me. Thus, over the past several years, and through access to previously top-secret cables and memoranda, I have been able to "eavesdrop" on Stasi spymaster Markus Wolf and KGB chairman Yuri Andropov as they speculated on the threat posed by the 1978 election of a Polish pope: speculations shaped by the reports of communist-bloc moles inside the Vatican. I have likewise been able to "sit in" on negotiations between the Polish communist government and the Holy See on the terms and conditions of John Paul's second pastoral visit to his homeland; and I have been able to "watch" an effort by the *Służba Bezpieczeństwa* (or SB, the Polish secret police) to influence those negotiations by trying to blackmail the pope. These newly available materials also shed light on Vatican diplomacy's efforts to find a modus vivendi with communist governments, even as those governments were intensifying their efforts to penetrate the Vatican.

It's all the stuff of great espionage fiction. Yet it happened. The way the communist war against Catholicism was conducted, the forms of ecclesiastical resistance to it that failed, and the resistance strategies that succeeded all contain important lessons for the future, even as they clarify the immediate past. That past commands attention and respect because of the vast human sacrifices it entailed. It also commands our attention for what it can teach about twenty-first-century Catholicism's engagement with new threats to religious freedom.

In a dinner conversation in late 1996, Pope John Paul II's longtime secretary, Stanisław Dziwisz, said, when speaking of the Catholic Church's struggle against communism in Poland, "You must understand that it was *always* 'them' and us.' " That is, the struggle between communism and Catholicism was not a matter of episodic confrontations, nor could it be understood by analogy to a parliamentary government and its opposition. It was all war, all the time.

That was certainly the communist view of the matter. From the beginnings of the Bolshevik Revolution, the leaders of Soviet communism regarded the Catholic Church as a mortal threat to their program and their interests. To Lenin and his successors (including Yuri Andropov, the only KGB chairman to become leader of the USSR), the Catholic Church was a vast, wealthy, unscrupulous international conspiracy whose aims included the demise of communism and the destruction of the workers' state. In the post–World War II period, when the United States was known in KGB circles as the "Main Adversary," the Catholic Church was understood to be a formidable ideological adversary. Its influence was feared for what it could do to the Soviet position in various countries of the Warsaw Pact. Its historic cultural links to nationalist sentiment in Lithuania and Ukraine threatened Stalin's inner empire. And it was known to be a principal obstacle to Soviet global objectives, including the export of Marxist-Leninist revolution to the Third World, especially Latin America.

The communist war against Catholicism intensified exponentially in the last years of World War II as the NKVD (predecessor of the KGB) sought to change the mentality of the populations of the central and eastern European countries that were to be brought into the Soviet orbit. It was in these years, for example, that the black legend of Pius XII's alleged indifference to the fate of European Jewry and his alleged sympathies for German

National Socialism was manufactured and disseminated by the Soviet intelligence service. Destroying the reputation of the pope and the Church was thought useful in preparing the ground for the triumph of the new socialist man east of the Elbe River.

In this season of brutality, clergy and consecrated religious men and women throughout the new Soviet outer empire were subjected to harassment, imprisonment, and death, mere months after being liberated from their Nazi torturers. Some of the surviving resistance heroes of the first decade of the communist assault on religious liberty are reasonably well known: the Polish primate, Stefan Wyszyński, who led that intensely Catholic country's vigorous resistance to communist attempts to make the Church a subsidiary of the Polish United Workers Party; Hungarian primate Jozef Mindszenty the living symbol of his people's crushed hopes after Soviet tanks ground down the 1956 Hungarian Revolution; Czech primate Josef Beran, who survived three Nazi concentration camps only to be imprisoned by the Czechoslovak communist regime; the Croatian leader of Yugoslav Catholicism, Alojzije Stepinac, who, like Mindszenty, endured a classic show trial and who was eventually martyred; the Slovak Jesuit, Ján Chryzostom Korec, clandestinely consecrated a bishop in 1951 at twenty-seven, who spent three decades conducting an underground ministry that frequently landed him in labor camps. The most brutal communist campaign against the Catholic Church in the immediate postwar period is not so well-known, however.

It involved the Greek Catholic Church of Ukraine, Byzantine in its liturgy and polity but in full communion with the bishop of Rome. Feared by Stalin as the repository of Ukrainian national consciousness and hated by the leadership of Russian Orthodoxy for their adhesion to Rome, the Greek Catholics were caught in a political-ecclesiastical vise that closed on them with lethal force in 1946, when an illegal Sobor, or church council, was held in

L'viv in western Ukraine. Staged by the Soviet secret police with the blessing of Russian Orthodoxy's Moscow patriarchate, the L'viv Sobor dissolved the 1596 Union of Brest, which had brought Ukrainian Greek Catholics into full communion with Rome, and announced that this local church had been "reunited" with Russian Orthodoxy. In one stroke, four million Ukrainian Greek Catholics who declined "reunion" with Russian Orthodoxy became the largest illegal, and underground, religious body in the world. Thousands of Greek Catholics, including numerous priests and all but two of ten Ukrainian Greek Catholic bishops, died in the Gulag.

By the late 1950s, a rough if variegated status quo had been established between the Catholic Church and communism throughout the Warsaw Pact. The Polish Church was getting stronger under Cardinal Wyszyński's leadership. Hungarian Catholicism was severely weakened by the failed uprising of 1956, while the Church in Czechoslovakia, often functioning underground, was under constant, brutal pressure. The Greek Catholics of Ukraine were worshipping in forests, where they also conducted clandestine schools and seminaries. The Latin-rite Catholics of Lithuania were holding out against relentless campaigns of both Russification and secularization. It was, as Stanisław Dziwisz said, *always* "them and us."

The election of Angelo Roncalli as Pope John XXIII in 1958 marked the beginning of a new phase of this war. Roncalli was concerned that the Church had experienced a certain sclerosis in the latter years of Pius XII. In the first decade of his pontificate, Pius XII had been something of a reformer, encouraging the liturgical movement, giving new impetus to Catholic biblical studies, and trying to get the Church to think of itself in biblical and theological, rather than canonical and legal, categories. If these tentative movements toward reform were to take hold, Roncalli believed, the energies they represented should be focused through an ecumenical council. This papal concern for the renewal of Catholicism's internal life quickly bumped up against the problem of the communist war against the Church: How were the bishops behind the Iron Curtain to participate in the Second Vatican Council?

This turned out to be less of a problem than anticipated, because the KGB and its sister intelligence services throughout the Warsaw Pact saw Vatican II as a golden opportunity to penetrate the Vatican, deploy new intelligence assets throughout Catholic institutions in Rome, and use the council's deliberations as a means of strengthening their own grip on restive Catholic populations behind the Iron Curtain. John XXIII's concerns about central and eastern European participation at Vatican II, and the new pope's conviction that it was time to test the possibility of a less frozen relationship between the Holy See and Moscow, combined to give birth to what was known as the Vatican's new *Ostpolitik*. The *Ostpolitik*, in turn, seemed even more urgent when the opening of Vatican II coincided with the Cuban Missile Crisis. Where the pope and the Vatican sought a new dialogue in the interests of world peace, however, the KGB and other Soviet-bloc intelligence agencies sought a new beachhead inside Vatican City in their war against the Catholic Church. The atmosphere of cordial hospitality extended by the Holy See to observers and "separated brethren" at the council created an ideal atmosphere for this communist effort to penetrate the Church's central administration.

Perhaps the most dramatic Soviet-bloc attempt to manipulate the work of Vatican II involved an old nemesis, Cardinal Wyszyński of Poland. During its first two working periods, the Council had debated how it should discuss the Blessed Virgin

Mary—through a separate document or by incorporating a reflection on Mary's role in salvation history into the Dogmatic Constitution on the Church? Colonel Stanisław Morawski, the director of Department IV of the Polish secret intelligence service, charged with anti-Church activities, saw in these theological debates an opportunity to damage Wyszyński's reputation in the world episcopate. So, working with theologians who were SB collaborators, Morawski prepared a memorandum charging Wyszyński with doctrinally dubious views of Mary. The memorandum, "On Selected Aspects of the Cult of the Virgin Mary in Poland," was circulated to all the bishops attending Vatican II, widely distributed in Europe, and regarded as authentic by journalists covering the Council. The Polish primate's standing at Vatican II was at least temporarily weakened.

The manipulation of theological debates for political ends was but one of the methods used by Soviet-bloc intelligence services during Vatican II. From the beginning of the Council's preparatory phase, Polish secret intelligence monitored the work of the Council's preparatory commissions and conducted operations against Polish participants at the Council, including electronic and other forms of surveillance, and intensified efforts to recruit collaborators. One well-placed Polish secret police collaborator in Rome, Father Michał Czajkowski (code-named JANKOWSKI), worked with the SB chief at the Polish embassy in Rome and directly with SB Department IV in Warsaw to furnish the secret police and the Polish communist government with regular reports. The evolution of conciliar texts touching on social and political matters was of obvious interest to Czajkowski's spymasters, but so was the development of ecumenical and interreligious dialogue, in which communist intelligence services saw new opportunities to create trouble, sow the seeds of division, and weaken local churches.

. . .

The Second Vatican Council ran parallel to the first years of the Vatican *Ostpolitik*, whose principal diplomatic agent was the Italian curialist Agostino Casaroli. In his memoirs, Casaroli described the countries of the Warsaw Pact in the early 1960s as a "vast, immobile swamp" that had "finally begun to ripple, though only lightly, under the winds of history." In Casaroli's view (and, one may assume, that of John XXIII and Paul VI), that immobility could not be blamed solely on the animosity of the Kremlin and its satellites; it also reflected the confrontational approach of Pius XII, whose sharp anticommunist statements allowed the communist authorities to treat any contacts with the Vatican by citizens of Soviet-bloc countries—such as bishops—as acts of espionage. Casaroli also believed that the 1949 Holy Office decree banning Catholic participation in communist parties under pain of excommunication was taken by communists to be an ongoing "declaration of war."

Casaroli, John XXIII, and Paul VI were also worried about the internal life of the Church behind the Iron Curtain, which, as Casaroli later wrote, was being "suffocated by the coils of a hostile power," such that it would eventually "succumb to a 'natural death.' " The prevent this, provision had to be made for the Church's sacramental life: that required priests; ordaining priests required bishops; and getting bishops in place required agreements with communist governments. So it was thought necessary to find a *modus non moriendi*, as Casaroli put it, a "way of not dying" until such time, perhaps long in the future, when the Cold War would dissolve as a liberalizing Soviet bloc met an increasingly social-democratic West.

From the communist point of view, however, the *Ostpolitik* and the general atmosphere of Vatican openness during the Council provided welcome opportunities to penetrate the Holy See while continuing the work of disintegrating the Catholic Church inside the Warsaw Pact. Thus Casaroli's initial agreement with the Kadar government in Hungary was used by that regime to take control of the Catholic Church in Hungary. Most bishops nominated under the 1964 Vatican-Hungarian agreement cooperated with Hungary's internal security and foreign intelligence services; by 1969, the Hungarian bishops' conference was in large measure controlled by the Hungarian state. So was the Pontifical Hungarian Institute in Rome, all of whose rectors in the late 1960s and half of whose students were trained agents of Hungarian secret intelligence. Roman collaborators who informed their masters in Budapest of Vatican negotiating positions from 1963 on put Vatican diplomats in very disadvantageous positions in their ongoing work with the Kadar regime. The most accomplished of these moles, Fritz Kuzen (MOZART), was an employee of Vatican Radio; MOZART helped prepare Hungarian negotiators for years, not least in efforts to get Cardinal Mindszenty out of his internal exile in the American embassy in Budapest.

Even as the *Ostpolitik*'s early years ran parallel to intensified Soviet persecution of independent elements within the Russian Orthodox Church (ROC), the Soviet government concurrently gave permission for the ROC to be officially represented at the World Council of Churches in Geneva—another opportunity, as the KGB saw it, for disseminating disinformation and propaganda while deploying agents of influence to blunt criticism of the repression of religious freedom behind the Iron Curtain. Later in the 1960s, the *Ostpolitik* succeeded in gaining permission for a few Lithuanian Catholics to study in Rome. Two Lithuanian KGB agents, ANTANAS and VIDMANTAS, studied at the Gregorian University, while two others, DAKTARAS and ZHIBUTE, participated in meetings of the Vatican commission charged with the reform of canon law.

In 1969, KGB chairman Andropov authorized a new series of active measures against the Vatican, aimed at convincing the Holy See to cease its "subversive activity." KGB assets in the ROC with good Vatican contacts (including the agents DROZDOV—the future Patriarch Aleksi II—and ADAMANT—Metropolitan Nikodim, who would die in the arms of Pope John Paul II in 1978) were instructed to "cause dissension between Vatican organizations such as the Congregations for the Eastern Church[es], the Secretariat for Christian Unity, and the Commission for Justice and Peace." ADAMANT was also ordered to warn his curial contacts that he feared the Soviet government would establish autonomous Catholic churches, "independent" of Rome, throughout the USSR. During this same period, the KGB intensified its efforts to destroy the underground Ukrainian Greek Catholic Church, charging one of its leaders, Volodomyr Sterniuk, with sexual improprieties; those charges were also leaked to the Vatican.

All war, all the time, indeed.

Prior to his election as pope, Karol Wojtyła was the object of intense scrutiny by both the Polish SB and the Soviet KGB. Like every other seminarian and priest in postwar Poland, Wojtyła had an SB file and an SB watcher from the outset of his ecclesiastical life; the file thickened and the number of watchers intensified after Wojtyła's consecration in 1958 as auxiliary bishop of Kraków. During the next twenty years, the SB came to loathe and fear Wojtyła even more than they feared Cardinal Wyszyński. It was not a question of Wyszyński losing his edge; rather, the dance between Wyszyński and the regime was one with which both sides were familiar. With Wojtyła, the regime never knew what might happen. And as the archbishop of Kraków found his voice as a defender of the human rights of all, he came to be seen as an even greater threat than Wyszyński.

In November 1973, the SB's Department IV created "Independent Group D," which was assigned the task of "distintegrating" Polish Catholicism through a coordinated attack on the Church's integrity. The leader of Independent Group D, SB colonel Konrad Straszewski, had been the secret-police contact of one of Wojtyła's colleagues at the Catholic University of Lublin for years. The reports on Wojtyła from Straszewski and other SB agents led Polish prosecutors to consider charging the archbishop of Kraków with sedition on three occasions in 1973–1974. Things had changed since the heyday of Polish Stalinism, however, and communist leader Edward Gierek did not dare do to Wojtyła what his predecessors had done to Wyszyński in 1953. So the surveillance of the archbishop increased, as did the efforts to suborn his associates in the archdiocesan chancery. And then there was the brutality: Msgr. Andrzej Bardecki, ecclesiastical advisor to the lay-run Catholic newspaper *Tygodnik Powszechny*, was beaten senseless by SB (or SB-inspired) thugs one night after leaving an editorial meeting that Cardinal Wojtyła also attended. Visiting the elderly priest in the hospital the next day, the archbishop said, "You replaced me; you were beaten instead of me." (Interestingly enough, the SB never attempted to suborn Wojtyła's close lay friends, thus exhibiting a peculiar communist form of clericalism.)

The SB did not discover the clandestine ordinations of priests for underground service in Czechoslovakia that Cardinal Wojtyła conducted in Kraków. But the secret police did know about, and could not have been pleased by, the archbishop's increasingly close contacts with lay (and often agnostic) Polish political dissidents in the mid-1970s. At a 1975 KGB-organized conference of Soviet bloc intelligence agencies, summoned to plan further anti-Vatican activities, the Polish, Hungarian, and Czechoslovak secret services all reported "significant agent positions" in the

Vatican, while the Hungarians warned that Wojtyła would be an especially dangerous opponent as pope.

Yuri Andropov evidently agreed. Shortly after the election of Pope John Paul II on October 16, 1978, the KGB sent several clandestine agents, known in the trade as "illegals," into Poland to gather what intelligence they could. One of them, Oleg Petrovich Buryen (DEREVLYOV), posed as the representative of a Canadian publishing company interested in Polish missionaries in Asia and made an assiduous effort to cultivate the new pope's old friend and fellow-philosopher Fr. Józef Tischner. The Polish SB, for its part, marked their countryman's election as bishop of Rome by deploying to the Eternal City a particularly sophisticated agent, Edward Kotowski (PIETRO), who, for the previous three years, had been given intense Italian-language training and told to learn everything he could about the Holy See and its ways. Working clandestinely under the cover of a diplomatic posting at the Polish embassy in Rome, PIETRO cultivated an extensive network of Vatican contacts, including men who had at least some access to the papal apartment. PIETRO later told Polish historian Andrzej Grajewski that, during the early years of John Paul II's pontificate, more than half of the "diplomats" working at the Polish embassy in Rome were in fact working for the SB, as were Rome-based employees of the Polish state airline and travel agency, members of the Polish trade mission to Italy, and various "illegals."

John Paul II suspected that the Holy See had been penetrated by Soviet-bloc intelligence and changed the papal routine to provide some measure of counterintelligence capacity. Materials dealing with Poland and other sensitive matters were no longer archived for ready reference in the Secretariat of State; rather, they were kept in the papal apartment, where there was no chance for mischief-makers to prowl about. John Paul also declined to dictate memoranda of conversations with notables such as Soviet foreign minister Andrei Gromyko, evidently concerned that such notes might fall into the wrong hands somewhere along the curial paper trail. So he and his secretary, Stanisław Dziwisz, got together every night to review the day's appointments and conversations, Dziwisz keeping notes in a series of diaries that remained under his control in the papal apartment.

Of particular interest throughout Soviet-bloc intelligence was the proposed papal visit to Poland in June 1979. Prior to the visit, the Polish SB mounted an enormous damage-limitation operation, LATO-79 (Summer-79), which managed to insert at least one clerical mole into the Church's planning commission for the papal visit. On this occasion, the SB worked in close collaboration with the Stasi, whose legendary spymaster, Markus Wolf, had his own intelligence asset in the Vatican: a German Benedictine, Eugen Brammertz (LICHTBLICK), who worked for the German edition of *L'Osservatore Romano*. While the pope was in Poland, igniting a revolution of conscience that quickly spread throughout the region, the SB deployed 480 agents in Kraków alone to monitor events and cause what trouble they could.

The intensity of concern displayed by the SB and the Stasi before and during the June 1979 papal pilgrimage was matched in Moscow, where the KGB charged the Polish pope with "ideological subversion." Moscow was particularly upset that John Paul had referred to himself as a "Slav pope"; this led the Soviet communist party's Politburo to conclude, in what would have been a surprise to Vatican diplomats, that the Holy See had launched a new "ideological struggle against the socialist countries." Five months later, the Central Committee secretariat of the Soviet communist party approved a six-point plan, entitled "Decision to Work Against the Policies of the Vatican in Relation with Socialist States," which included an active-measures campaign in the West to "demonstrate that the leadership of the new pope, John

Paul II, is dangerous to the Catholic Church." In this context, "active measures" meant propaganda, disinformation campaigns, blackmail, and an attempt to persuade the world press that the pope was a threat to peace. Soviet fears intensified by an order of magnitude the following year with the rise of the Solidarity movement—an enterprise that Yuri Andropov immediately sought to influence through the infiltration of more "illegals" into Poland. The pope's warning against an anti-Solidarity Soviet invasion of Poland in December 1980 added yet another item to the bill of indictment that eventually was served on John Paul by Mehmet Ali Agca on May 13, 1981.

The failed assassination attempt was not the end of the communist war against John Paul II, however. That war took a nasty turn during the difficult negotiations preceding the second papal pilgrimage to Poland in June 1983, when the country was still under martial law. Eager to gain the upper hand, the SB decided to blackmail John Paul. The instrument chosen was a fake diary, said to have been written by a deceased former employee of the archdiocese of Kraków during Wojtyła's archbishopric, in which the "diarist," Irina Kinaszewska, reported that she had been the archbishop's lover. The plot unraveled when Grzegorz Piotrowski of Independent Group D, the man charged with planting the fake diary in the home of a prominent Cracovian priest, got roaring drunk after the successful break-in, crashed his car, and told the traffic police what he had been up to. Word of the plot began to leak out of police circles, as it did from the Kraków chancery when the fake diary was discovered and recognized for what it was. Thus the plot to blackmail the pope self-destructed.

The diary affair has something of the feel of the Keystone Kops about it—until one recognizes just how deeply the SB (and the Polish government) feared John Paul II, even in a country under martial law, and how low they were prepared to sink in order to undermine his moral authority. As for Captain Piotrowski, he would reappear a year and a half later—as the man who beat Father Jerzy Popiełuszko to death and dumped his battered body into the Vistula River.

All war, all the time.

It will be decades, perhaps centuries, before the full story of the communist war against the Catholic Church is told. Yet given the new availability of materials from communist governmental and secret police archives, some lessons from this struggle can be suggested. The first involves the nature of the conflict.

Catholicism and communism offered the world two radically different visions of human nature, human community, human origins, and human destiny. These visions were fundamentally incompatible, which explains in part the ferocity of the animus communism directed against the Church. That incompatibility also suggests that the strategic vision of John Paul II, which encompassed the victory of freedom over totalitarian tyranny, was more acute than those who imagined a slow convergence between liberalizing communism and an increasingly social-democratic West. There would be no convergence here. Someone was going to win and someone was going to lose. As it happened, the truth about the human person proved its strength over time. The sacrifice of the martyrs reminds us that that proving involved severe testing and great heroism.

This truth about the nature of the conflict bears reflection when considering the threats to religious freedom and other basic human rights posed by China, Vietnam, North Korea, and Cuba, and by jihadist Islamism (which, in power, takes on many of the characteristics of Western totalitarianism). What lessons might be drawn from experience of the Vatican *Ostpolitik* in the 1960s and 1970s for the Church's relations with China, Vietnam, and Cuba today? What lessons might be drawn from that experience for the Church's struggle to survive in the Arab Islamic world? And, to press the question into territory where Western political leaders do not want to go, does the Church's experience vis-à-vis communism offer lessons about the twenty-first-century Church's relationship to aggressive, exclusivist secularism and its attempts to establish what Pope Benedict XVI has called a "dictatorship of relativism"?

In reflecting on those questions, it should be recognized that the Catholic attempt to find a modus vivendi (or, in Cardinal Casaroli's term, *modus non moriendi*) with communist powers rarely, if ever, paid significant dividends. In fact, the problem of the Church's relationship with political systems that attempt to fill all space in society long antedates the rise of Russian Bolshevism. Appeasement did not work with Napoleon; it did not work with Mexican or Spanish anti-clerical regimes; it did not work in post-*Anschluss* Austria; so it should not have been a surprise that it did not work with communism.

The most poignant of the *Ostpolitik*'s failures was in Hungary, where the Church's integrity was gravely compromised by the post-Mindszenty episcopal leadership and its acquiescence to the Hungarian communist regime; the effects of that failure are still felt today. The countercase to Hungary was Poland, where history will judge Cardinal Wyszyński a better strategist and tactician than the architects of the Vatican *Ostpolitik*. Resistance, unapologetic and unrelenting, helped keep Catholicism alive in Lithuania and Ukraine; acquiescence and appeasement were destroying the Church in Bohemia and Moravia until John Paul II inspired the octogenarian Cardinal František Tomášek to become a resistance hero in the 1980s.

Successful resistance, in turn, was based on a strong sense of

Catholic identity, coupled with the kind of political shrewdness displayed by Stefan Wyszyński and Karol Wojtyła—a shrewdness that combined steadiness of strategic vision with tactical flexibility. Wyszyński's attempts to find space for the Polish Church to recover its strength after World War II were not always appreciated by the Vatican of the late 1940s, where the strategic vision was clear—communism must be defeated—but the tactical circumstances in Poland were not so well understood. The situation was reversed in the 1970s, with the Vatican urging tactical flexibility (aimed at establishing formal diplomatic relations between the Holy See and the Polish People's Republic) while Wyszyński took a tactical hard line, correctly fearing communist efforts to play divide-and-conquer, with the diplomats of the Holy See as unwitting pawns on the chessboard.

For his part, Karol Wojtyła, Pope John Paul II, was shrewd enough to understand that appointing the architect of Paul VI's *Ostpolitik*, Agostino Casaroli, as his own secretary of state created tactical advantages for the Church. As the pope preached moral revolution over the heads of communist regimes, speaking directly to their people, Casaroli continued his diplomacy, thus denying the communists the opportunity to charge that the Church had reneged on its commitment to dialogue. It cannot be said that Cardinal Casaroli's memoirs reveal any great appreciation for this division of labor. In fact, Casaroli's 1990 praise of Mikhail Gorbachev as the pivotal figure in the Revolution of 1989—in a lecture in Kraków, no less—suggests that this ablest of Vatican diplomats never really grasped the full genius of John Paul II's approach. Still, John Paul and Casaroli made a formidable team, if not precisely in the way Casaroli (who once said, wistfully, that "I would like to help this pope but 1 find him so different") would have wanted.

The Catholic Church's experience with Soviet communism may also hold lessons for the Church's relationship with Russian Orthodoxy and the Russian state today. Russian Orthodoxy counts many thousands of noble martyrs among its twentieth-century gifts to God. Yet from the end of the Second World War through the collapse of the USSR, the Russian Orthodox leadership was largely a subsidiary of the KGB. The 1974 "Furov Report" by the Soviet Council on Religious Affairs distinguished three categories of Russian Orthodox bishops: the first category included those "who affirm in word and deed not only loyalty but patriotism towards the socialist society; strictly observe the laws on cults, and educate the parish clergy and believers in the same spirit; realistically understand that our state is not interested in proclaiming the role of religion and the Church in society; and, realizing this, do not display any particular activeness in extending the influence of Orthodoxy among the population." The bishops in this category included Patriarch Pimen, who refused to invite John Paul II to Moscow for the 1988 celebration of the millennium of Christianity among the eastern Slavs, and Patriarch Aleksi II, the successor to Pimen who refused to allow John Paul II to come to post-communist Russia.

Patriarch Pimen's praise for the "lofty spiritual qualities" of Yuri Andropov, chief persecutor of Soviet Christians for decades, is an example at the outer boundaries of toadying to power. But praise for the czar of the day is not an anomaly in Russian Orthodoxy history. That pattern of collaboration continues today with the current patriarch, Kirill, whose support for the revanchism of Vladimir Putin has put a considerable strain on relations between the ROC, on the one hand, and the Ukrainian Greek Catholic and Ukrainian Orthodox communities in Ukraine, on the other. Kirill's appointment as an ROC representative to the World

Council of Churches in Geneva when he was a twenty-five-year-old newly ordained priest could not have been anything other than the work of the KGB. One hopes that this intelligent, sophisticated man has disengaged himself from his previous political entanglements. But the early years of his patriarchate, with their insistence on certain territories being the exclusive cultural sphere of Russian Orthodoxy, have not been reassuring. Thus perhaps the time has come for the Catholic–Russian Orthodox dialogue to focus on certain basic questions of Church-state relations. Proposals by the Moscow Patriarchate for a joint Catholic–Russian Orthodox "new evangelization" in Europe will likely lie fallow until a mutual baseline of understanding about the proper relationship of Christian churches to state authority, and about the non-ethnically determined character of the free act of faith, has been established.

Finally, the ferocity of the communist assault on the Church, in which Christians were fed to wild animals and crucified for the first time since the days of Diocletian, offers an important lesson about ultramundane politics wedded to modern technology in societies devoid of transcendent moral reference points that provide a cultural check on state power. The slaughters of the European wars of religion took place almost four centuries ago; the far greater slaughters of twentieth-century communism took place within living memory. That historical fact might usefully be raised in Brussels, Washington, and various European capitals when alarms are sounded about the alleged dangers of religiously informed moral argument in the public square.

The communist war against Christianity was a bloody affair, in which Christian martyrdom reached new heights of sacrifice. That war also involved billions of man-hours of work and billions of dollars of public expenditure and was thus a form of theft from civil society. Deeply committed and politically shrewd Christian pastors and laity eventually won out over communism. The blood of martyrs, however, was the seed of the Church's victory. Their sacrifice and what we can learn from it about the cardinal virtue of fortitude—courage—must never be forgotten.

CYNTHIA ZARIN

From The Book of Knowledge

FROM *The American Scholar*

(*The Children's Encyclopedia*/The Grolier Society, vol. 115, 1936)

1. What makes a fairy ring?

   Fairy rings are made of a kind of fungus.

2. Why does damp air make us ill?

   Damp air is often cold air, and the cold has usually been blamed for making us ill, though many facts prove that it is not blameworthy at all.

3. Why does a dog go round and round before it lies down?

   The answer to this question lies in another question. What is a dog?

4. Can our brains ever fill up?

   The poet Browning says "there is no end to learning."

5. Why does a tuning fork sound louder when it touches wood?

   The sound from a tuning fork, like the light from a candle, flows out in all directions.

6. Why are some things poisonous?
    *We could only answer this question completely and
    fully if we knew all there is to know about life.*

7. Why can we hear better when we shut our eyes?
    This question is partly true and partly not true.

8. Can an animal think?
    *There is no doubt an animal can think, and that it can
    remember.*

9. Do animals feel pain as we do?
    That is not a question that can be answered directly.

10. Why do we not growl like animals when we are
    hungry?
    A hungry man is an angry man.

11. Why have leaves different shapes?
    *The great idea which we learn to apply to every fact
    about living creatures is that these facts usually
    have uses.*

12. Why do the leaves of the aspen always shake?
    *The shaking of the leaves has the same effect as if
    the trees were fanning themselves.*

13. Why does oil make a wheel go round more easily?
    It all depends on where the oil is put.

14. Why do we see the stars only at night?
    *The stars are shining all the time, sending light to
    earth, but more than this is needed for us to see.*

15. Is an atom alive?

It is almost a living thing.

16. Can country people see "writ small" better than townspeople?

If country folk use their eyes mainly at distances, their vision will be keenest at distances.

17. Why does a lump rise in my throat when I cry?

It is the place of speech which is the most marvelous thing.

Contributors' Notes

Coleman Barks has most recently published *Rumi: The Big Red Book: The Great Masterpiece Celebrating Mystical Love and Friendship* and *Just Being Here: Rumi and Human Friendship*, a collaboration with David Darling (cello), a three-CD set.

Annie Boutelle, born in Scotland, holds the position of Poet in Residence at Smith College. Her new book of poetry is *This Caravaggio*.

Carl Dennis's many books include *Practical Gods* (Pulitzer Prize for Poetry, 2002) and, most recently, *Callings*.

Brian Doyle is the editor of *Portland Magazine* at the University of Portland in Oregon. He is the author of many books, most recently a "sprawling headlong epic moist Oregon novel," *Mink River*; a collection of short stories, *Bin Laden's Bald Spot & Other Stories*; and a collection of spiritual essays, *Grace Notes* (from ACTA Publications in Chicago), in which the essay "Let It Go" appears.

Terry Eagleton is Distinguished Professor of English Literature at the University of Lancaster and the author of many books, including, most recently, *Why Marx Was Right* and *On Evil*.

Adam Gopnik is a staff writer for *The New Yorker* and the author of *The Table Comes First: Family, France, and the Meaning of Food; Winter: Five Windows on the Season;* and other books.

Jessica Greenbaum is the poetry editor of *upstreet* and the author of *Inventing Difficulty*, a book of poems.

Malcolm Guite is a priest in the Church of England and chaplain at Girton College, University of Cambridge. He is the author of *What Do Christians Believe?: Belonging and Belief in Modern Christianity* and *Faith, Hope and Poetry: Theology and the Poetic Imagination*. He has published poetry in various journals and reviews including *Christianity and Literature, Radix*, and *Second Spring*.

Linda Heuman is an essayist and journalist and a contributing editor at *Tricycle: The Buddhist Review*. She has studied and practiced Buddhism in Asia and America over two decades and now writes about the transmission of Buddhism to the West. Her articles, essays, and reviews have also appeared in *Buddhadharma, Stanford Magazine, Plenty*, and *The Industry Standard*. She is based in Providence, Rhode Island.

Kathleen Hill teaches in the MFA program at Sarah Lawrence College. *Who Occupies This House*, her new novel, appeared in 2010 and was named an Editors' Choice in the *New York Times Book Review*. An earlier novel, *Still Waters in Niger*, was short-listed in its French translation for the Prix Femina Étranger and nominated for the Dublin IMPAC award.

Edward Hirsch is the author of many books of poetry and prose, most recently *The Living Fire: New and Selected Poems*.

Jane Hirshfield's many books include *Come, Thief: Poems; After: Poems;* and *The Heart of Haiku.*

Edward Hoagland is the author of many books of essays, travel, and fiction. His newest, *Alaskan Travels: Far-Flung Tales of Love and Adventure,* was published in 2012. His first, *Cat Man,* appeared fifty-six years ago.

Pico Iyer is the author of eight works of nonfiction, including *The Lady and the Monk: Four Seasons in Kyoto; The Global Soul: Jet Lag, Shopping Malls, and the Search for Home;* and *The Open Road: The Global Journey of the Fourteenth Dalai Lama;* and two novels. His most recent book is *The Man Within My Head,* an exploration of Graham Greene, conscience, and the power of compassionate realism.

Mark Jarman is Centennial Professor of English at Vanderbilt University. His latest collection of poetry is *Bone Fires: New and Selected Poems.*

Charles Johnson is a MacArthur Fellow and the author of the National Book Award–winning novel *Middle Passage.* He is professor emeritus at the University of Washington in Seattle.

James Lasdun is the author of several books of poetry and fiction, most recently *It's Beginning to Hurt,* a collection of stories.

Sy Montgomery is the author of seventeen books for adults and children, including *Birdology: Adventures with a Pack of Hens, a Peck of Pigeons, Cantankerous Crows, Fierce Falcons, Hip Hop Parrots, Baby Hummingbirds, and One Murderously Big Living Dinosaur* and *Journey of the Pink Dolphins: An Amazon Quest.*

Francesca Aran Murphy is professor of theology at the University of Notre Dame and the coeditor of *Theology, University, Humanities*. Her other books include *God Is Not a Story: Realism Revisited* and *Art and Intellect in the Philosophy of Etienne Gilson*.

David Novak holds the J. Richard and Dorothy Shiff Chair of Jewish Studies as professor of the study of religion and professor of philosophy at the University of Toronto. His many books include *In Defense of Religious Liberty* and *Tradition in the Public Square: A David Novak Reader*.

P. J. O'Rourke, the author of many best-selling books, is the H. L. Mencken Research Fellow at the Cato Institute. His recent books include *Holidays in Heck* and *Don't Vote It Just Encourages the Bastards*.

Vince Passaro teaches literature and creative writing at Adelphi University. He is the author of *Violence, Nudity, Adult Content: A Novel*.

Stephen Prothero is the author of *The American Bible: How Our Words Unite, Divide, and Define a Nation*, and a professor of religion at Boston University. He blogs for CNN's *Belief Blog* and has written for the *New York Times*, the *Wall Street Journal*, *Newsweek*, *USA Today*, the *Washington Post*, and other publications.

Melissa Range's first book of poems, *Horse and Rider*, won the 2010 Walt McDonald Prize in Poetry and was published by Texas Tech University Press. Her poems have appeared in *32*

Poems, Image, New England Review, and other literary journals. Originally from East Tennessee, she is currently pursuing her PhD in English at the University of Missouri.

Patrick Henry Reardon, a senior editor of *Touchstone: A Journal of Mere Christianity,* is the author of *Christ in the Psalms* and *The Jesus We Missed: The Surprising Truth About the Humanity of Christ.*

Marilynne Robinson, a novelist and essayist, is the author of many books, including *When I Was a Child I Read Books: Essays; Absence of Mind: The Dispelling of Inwardness from the Modern Myth of the Self; Home;* and *Gilead* (Pulitzer Prize for Fiction, 2005).

Abdullah Saeed is the Sultan of Oman Professor of Arab and Islamic Studies at the University of Melbourne, Australia. His essay includes material delivered in a lecture given to the James Madison Program at Princeton University.

Nicholas Samaras is from Patmos, Greece. He's also lived in England, Wales, Switzerland, Italy, Austria, Germany, Yugoslavia, Jerusalem, and thirteen states in the United States, and writes from a place of permanent exile. His first book, *Hands of the Saddlemaker,* won the Yale Series of Younger Poets Award and his work has appeared or is forthcoming in *The New Yorker, Poetry, The Paris Review,* the *New York Times, The New Republic, Kenyon Review,* and *Image.*

Algis Valiunas is a contributing editor at *The New Atlantis* and a fellow of the Ethics and Public Policy Center.

George Weigel is Distinguished Senior Fellow at the Ethics and Public Policy Center, where he holds the William E. Simon Chair in Catholic Studies. His most recent book is *The End and the Beginning: Pope John Paul II—the Victory of Freedom, the Last Years, the Legacy.*

Philip Zaleski is the editor of the Best Spiritual Writing series and the author of many books, most recently *Prayer: A History* and a forthcoming book on the Inklings (both with his wife Carol Zaleski). He is a research associate at Smith College.

Cynthia Zarin is the author of many books of poems, including *The Ada Poems* and *The Watercourse*, and five books for children. She teaches at Yale University.

Other Notable Spiritual Writing of the Year

Joseph Bottum, "God and the Detectives," *Books & Culture.*

Peter Cole, "From the Sky to the Heavens' Heavens,"
   Paris Review.

Robert Cording, "Elegy for an Idea," *The Georgia Review.*

Lillian Daniel, "You Can't Make This Up," *Christian Century.*

Mary Ann Glendon, "The Bearable Lightness of Being,"
   First Things.

Father Charles Gordon CSC, "Why I Am a Priest,"
   Portland.

John Hannam, "Modern Science's Christian Sources,"
   First Things.

Lisa Ohlen Harris, "The Game of Life," *River Teeth.*

John Herlihy, "The Metaphoric Ascent of Prayer," *Adyan
   Journal.*

Linda Hogan, "Snow," *Orion.*

Daniel Walker Howe, "Classical Education in America," *Wilson Quarterly.*

Lin Jensen, "Right Lying," *Tricycle.*

Mark Noll, "A World Without the King James Version," *Christianity Today.*

Nancy J. Nordenson, "Woman on Michigan Avenue," *Saint Katherine Review.*

Eugene H. Peterson, "My Father's Butcher Shop," *Christian Century.*

Mark Phillips, "Time Enough for a Story," *Notre Dame Magazine.*

Clark Strand, "13 Ways of Looking at a Madman," *Tricycle.*

David Wagoner, "Waiting by a River," *Bellevue Literary Review.*

C. R. Wiley, "Stirred by Shakers," *Touchstone.*

Meaghan Winter, "Orthodox Chic," *The Believer.*